EMPOWERED

Why We Need
Spirit-Filled
Churches

KIE BOWMAN
FOREWORD BY RONNIE FLOYD

Auxano
PRESS

ISBN: 978-0-615-19789-0

Published by Auxano Press, Travelers Rest, South Carolina,
www.AuxanoPress.com.

Cover design and Layout: CrosslinCreative.net
Images: vectorstock.com

Cover image: "The Descent of the Spirit" by Gustave Doré. Public
domain.

Scripture quotations are from the ESV® Bible (The Holy Bible,
English Standard Version®), copyright © 2001 by Crossway, a
publishing ministry of Good News Publishers. Used by permis-
sion. All rights reserved.

Printed in the United States of America

23 22 21 20 19—5 4 3 2 1

To my dear wife, Tina. From the day we met, she has made my life better. It is my constant desire to love her the way Christ loved the church. She deserves it!

"Her children rise up and call her blessed;
her husband also, and he praises her."
(Proverbs 31:28)

CONTENTS

ACKNOWLEDGMENTS

Some key people have uniquely contributed to the completion of this book, and I want to thank each of them.

I am blessed to have led the congregation of Hyde Park Baptist/The Quarries Church as pastor for more than twenty-one years. They inspire and encourage me with their deep commitment to making the gospel of Jesus Christ known and to helping believers grow in their spiritual lives.

Equally, the church's staff has been an encouragement and support throughout this project by enabling me to have the time I needed for research and writing. My very capable executive assistant, Becky Shipp, has helped as a proofreader. The cover art was developed by our graphic artist, Jeff Johnson. I am grateful for the support I have received from each one.

I am also grateful to Dr. Ken Hemphill and his team at Auxano Press, including Maleah Bell, who proofed and edited the manuscript, for the opportunity to partner with them as we work together to help people grow in their knowledge of the Word of God.

Additionally, I am indebted to a host of scholars and Christian leaders who have written about the Holy Spirit. While I have attempted to give credit where it is necessary, my thinking has undoubtedly been influenced over the years by many others. So my thoughts expressed as my own in this work have naturally been influenced by the thoughts of others.

Finally, Tina, my wife of thirty-seven-plus years, has been so willing and patient in allowing me the time to complete this work. I am ever grateful for her in so many ways.

FOREWORD

As the president of the National Day of Prayer task force and one of the recent past presidents of the Southern Baptist Convention, I have had the opportunity to meet personally many of America's greatest spiritual leaders, hear them speak, read their books, and pray with them. I believe one of the men God is raising up to speak to the church and to our nation today is Dr. J. Kie Bowman.

Kie has been a personal friend for many years, and God has been doing a mighty work within his heart and through his life over the past two decades. This fresh and mighty work is leading Kie to impact one of America's greatest cities, which happens to be the capital city of Texas. This local church pastor is living out the pages of this book in Austin. Kie is not an out-of-touch author who pontificates about church life in America. You are holding in your hands a book by an author who actually understands the church and has a heart for all of the 300,000 plus churches in America today.

Kie Bowman believes the church is on this earth to fulfill the Great Commission: presenting the gospel of Jesus Christ to every person in the world and to make disciples of all the nations. In his leading and preaching, and in his writings, he exudes this gospel-advancing obsession.

With this end result in mind, Dr. Bowman is fully aware that without the power of the Holy Spirit upon the church, gospel advancement will be limited or even nonexistent. That is why he believes we need Spirit-filled churches not just in America but across the globe.

An impotent church is an oxymoron to New Testament Christianity. For far too long America has seen what *humans* can do with the church; now is the time for America to see what *God* can do with and through His church! This is possible when pastors, Christian leaders, and churches are being filled and empowered with the Holy Spirit.

For this reason, I encourage you to read *Empowered: Why We Need Spirit-Filled Churches.* God's will for His church is for it to be empowered by the Spirit from on high. God wants His church to experience and ooze with spiritual life. He wants His church to be mobilized for the Great Commission locally, statewide, nationally, and internationally. This is only possible when the church is being filled with the Holy Spirit.

My friends, this is why Pastor Kie Bowman believes in the power of prayer and why the teaching of the Bible and the equipping of the saints to do the work of the ministry is a priority for him. Kie believes God wants all of His churches on this planet to be filled with the Holy Spirit.

May the Lord God of heaven use this book in your life and church in such a way that the world *will* begin to see what God wants to do through His church.

I believe.

Dr. Ronnie Floyd, senior pastor, Cross Church
Springdale, AR

INTRODUCTION

Interest in the ministry of the Holy Spirit surged during the twentieth century. Some, although definitely not all, of the focus was combative, as traditional churches resisted the teaching and emphasis of their charismatic counterparts. Fortunately, when Christians debate what it means to be Christian, we can turn to a reliable, authoritative, and objective source, rather than merely depending upon the opinions of those in the debate. We have the Bible. As a result of challenges to what we regard as settled doctrine, we are forced to dig deeper, to rethink and restate our beliefs. Often the debates strengthen our beliefs and our ability to express them in a way the tranquility of the status quo never could.

I grew up attending traditional Baptist churches where we knew about the Holy Spirit, but I don't recall hearing much about His ministry to believers or how we should interact with Him. On the other hand, for most of my life before my late teens, I wasn't too focused on *anything* I heard in church. That changed when the Jesus movement erupted in our hometown, particularly at my high school. The *Jesus freaks* talked about the Holy Spirit in ways I had never heard in my church.

When I finally started following Jesus, I also started reading the Bible and Christian biographies. It didn't take long before I sensed a disconnect between my limited understanding of the Holy Spirit and what I read in the New Testament.

As I continued to study, learn, and grow, I became interested in the German pietistic movement, the Wesleyan revival, the Great Awakening, Moody's and Torrey's teaching, the holiness movement, the Keswick movement, and more. The history of the church's explanation of the Holy Spirit has been, at times, a dynamic attempt and, often, a struggle to represent accurately the teaching of Scripture. In every generation, people of goodwill have come down on opposite sides of the various theological positions. Christians haven't always agreed, and that remains the case today.

This book is not about reconciling various branches of the church. Instead, it is one interpreter's honest belief that some crucial ministries of the Holy Spirit are taught clearly in the New Testament and must be understood and lived. After all, if the people who have descended from the movement birthed in the wind and fire of the upper room can't understand the Holy Spirit, who can?

Over the years, I've read, written, and taught on the subject of the Holy Spirit, and I've noticed a trend. In popular Evangelicalism, and in American charismatic teaching, the role of the Holy Spirit is frequently, if not predominantly, explained in terms of the individual believer's experience. Charismatic teaching on the baptism of the Holy Spirit, as well as the evangelical teaching on being filled with the Spirit, has usually tended to stress the personal experience of empowerment. This has been true of most sermons I've heard and most I've preached. The personal experience of the individual has also been the theme of much of what I've read and written.

A personal relationship with the Holy Spirit is absolutely essential to an effective and growing Christian life; however, the Holy Spirit has always been active beyond the experience of individuals. There are ministries of the Holy Spirit to the entire body of Christ that occur even when the individual experience of some believers is lacking. In other words, by God's grace, the

Holy Spirit is often at work in the church long before believers are aware of their need to be filled with the Spirit. Most of what the Spirit does is a ministry to the entire church—not merely to those who seek a deeper touch of the Spirit's presence in their personal lives.

Emphasizing one aspect of the Spirit's ministry and activity does not have to mean de-emphasizing the other aspects of His work. *Empowered: Why We Need Spirit-Filled Churches* is about both the Spirit's ministry to the entire body *and* His ministry to the individual believer. Every individual believer should be Spirit-filled; and every church should recognize the work of the Spirit in its midst, even if some of the members are not Spirit-filled.

A basic premise of this book is woven throughout the chapters in both overt and subtle ways: the church is lifeless and essentially useless apart from the life-giving power of the Holy Spirit. Every pastor, teacher, and leader should be constantly comparing the church in Acts to our own churches and asking the Holy Spirit to bridge the gap between how the church started and what it is today. I read somewhere that Jesus started the church the way He wanted it; now He wants the church the way He started it.

My prayer is that this book will contribute to our understanding of the Spirit's ministry to the entire body of Christ and ignite a passion for a fresh anointing of the Holy Spirit's power in our individual lives.

J. Kie Bowman
Austin, Texas
December, 2018

"These things God has revealed to us through the Spirit. For the Spirit searches everything, even the depths of God." (1 Cor. 2:10)

THE SPIRIT EMPOWERS THE CHURCH

Luke 24:44-49; Acts 1:3-9

I remember the day American soldiers surrounded the hole in the ground where Saddam Hussein was hiding. The tyrannical dictator didn't look so brash and intimidating when he was caught living like a mole—hunkered down in a filthy, underground space only barely more impressive than a grave.

About three years after the discovery of the *Butcher of Baghdad* hiding in the hole, Hussein was tried, convicted, and hanged for his reign of terror against his own people; but why?

The reasons why Saddam Hussein was found guilty are obvious, but why did he find himself being put on trial? Why did he end up living in a hole in the desert floor? Why didn't Hussein submit to United Nations inspections to rule out the possibility he was amassing weapons of mass destruction? After all, wasn't the suspected presence of weapons of mass destruction and Hussein's unwillingness to comply with United Nations inspections one of the leading justifications for the United States' invasion of Iraq? And hasn't history demonstrated that Hussein, as evil as he was, apparently had no weapons of mass destruction? So, why did he not come clean? Why did he not do everything he could to avoid war with America?

The answer has to do with power. For Saddam Hussein, who began threatening people with guns when he was still a child, and who brutally murdered his political opponents to achieve and maintain power, the only thing that mattered was power. That, however, was the problem. He didn't really have any military power; at least, in his mind, not enough power. Iraq had no nukes. His army was an undisciplined, disloyal, antiquated mockery of a military. He had only one form of power: a big bluff. He had to maintain the threat that he had stockpiles of weapons of mass destruction for as long as he could, but who was he kidding? From his devious and twisted perspective, the United States, as it turns out, was not his biggest threat.

His huge neighbor and enemy to the east, Iran, was getting more powerful and threatening by the hour, and Saddam apparently feared what would happen if Iran realized he did not possess weapons of mass destruction. Power was so important to him that even the illusion of power was better than no power at all.[1]

In the end, Saddam's lust for power was his undoing; or, perhaps more accurately, his fear of being powerless was his biggest weakness. Either way, as it turns out in a perverse way, Saddam was right. Power was everything for him because, without it, he was done—finished. If he didn't have power, he needed the illusion of power. With neither, he ultimately ended up living like a rat in a miserable hole in the desert floor and finally died on a crudely constructed hangman's gallows at the end of a thick, short rope. It was the end of Saddam but neither the beginning nor the end of man's strange relationship and obsession with power.

The Right Power

Of course, it's true that power in the wrong hands and used for the wrong reasons usually becomes a threat and, sometimes, something worse. Perhaps Lord John Dalberg-Acton was mostly correct when he said, "Power tends to corrupt, and absolute power corrupts absolutely."[2] On the other end of the spectrum, however, we rely happily on power every day, and our lives are doubtlessly better for it. Power keeps hospitals open and emergency medical vehicles rushing to accident scenes. Power keeps our homes cool in the southern summers and warm in the northern winters. Almost everything we do depends upon some form of external power. We need power, and no one can reasonably deny that.

For instance, I once had a job selling electric generators in Alaska, and one day a young couple wandered into the showroom to consider buying one. They lived in the interior Alaskan *bush*—a vast and mostly unpopulated, rural area separated from any US highway or road system and, at least in those days, often without electricity. The young couple I met that day was ready to upgrade. After settling on a large, portable generator that was capable of producing substantial power, we sat down to finish the paperwork for the sale. I will never forget when the man suddenly turned to the lady and asked sincerely, "Are you sure you want to do this? You can get spoiled with electricity." She assured him she was willing to take that risk. The young lady was ready for power!

The truth is obvious: power in the hands of good people isn't a problem. In fact, in many instances the lack of power is the bigger challenge. It was, in fact, a deficiency of power that concerned Jesus most about leaving His infant church alone after His resurrection and ascension to heaven. Would the church be able to carry on His bold mission in His absence? No, they wouldn't. Not on their own, anyway. They needed additional support and outside resources beyond their individual or collective capacity. They needed a power surge, and so do we.

The Church's First Energy Crisis

The first followers of Jesus were usually broke. Jesus once had to resort to catching a fish with a mouthful of money in order to pay their taxes (Matt. 17:27). They lacked any political influence; their religious leaders considered them a dangerous cult and, therefore, had turned against them. Perhaps worst of all, they really didn't know what they didn't know. To add to the growing immensity of their overwhelmed lives, within days of the resurrection, Jesus gathered His little group of followers and laid out a master plan of world evangelization that was humanly impossible—then and now.

Fortunately, Jesus never intended for His church to operate in its own strength; even though we can frequently exercise impressive commitment and, at times, collectively appear expertly trained and financially stable. But we are not making the dent in the darkness we need to make, and we know it.

The twenty-first-century church now counts followers who number in the billions, educates students worldwide, and sends missionaries to unreached people groups. We have megachurches, hospitals, universities, television networks, and publishing companies. The picture of the church today obviously isn't all bad; in fact, in some cases it's incredible. Still, especially in the West, we sense the growing absence of our spiritual influence on our own culture.

Jesus never intended for His church to operate in its own strength.

Could the problem be in our message? I don't think so; at least not in every case. After all, the twentieth century saw a proliferation of Bible translations and scholarship as well as a renewed focus on biblical inerrancy. Millions of Christians in America love the Bible and enjoy an abundance of excellent Bible teaching. While we once traveled to other cities to hear the best Bible teachers in conferences, now the best of the best are a keystroke away, online twenty-four hours a day. We have never had access to so much quality teaching on a wide range of subjects. So, what is missing?

The vision Jesus had in mind for the church has always required more than good teaching. Even the best teaching is not quite enough. For instance, consider the original disciples' theological education. No students have ever had a better teacher than Jesus of Nazareth, have they? Each of the apostles had graduated from the *First Christian Seminary*, which specialized in in-depth teaching, hands-on experience, and personal interaction with Jesus—their only professor. Yet, He did not send them out to do ministry based on their unique educational advantages alone. If *they* didn't know enough to take the gospel to the world, why do we mistakenly think another class or degree is enough to send *our* generation into the battle? I am a believer in training and biblical education. I spent all of my twenties pursuing advanced degrees and have taught the Bible ever since. Education alone, however, is insufficient and inevitably falls short of the strategy Jesus envisioned.

In addition, the first disciples were eyewitnesses to Jesus's ministry. But that still wasn't enough. They knew He was crucified on Friday morning, died on Friday afternoon, and was alive again on Sunday. For them, the resurrection wasn't merely a cherished doctrinal position they subscribed to. They were there; it was part of their personal experience.

No preacher has ever had a more compelling personal testimony than each of the apostles. After everything they had seen, they must have been bursting at the seams with eagerness to tell people about Jesus. Surprisingly, however, even with all they carried in their ministerial toolbox, the Lord said, "Wait." They still were not ready (Luke 24:49).

What more could they possibly have needed? They lacked one thing: *power*. Powerlessness is the crippling deficiency the church frequently fails to consider. Candidly, many of us want financial power, denominational power, and political power. That kind of power makes good sense to us and those around us. The early church had none of that, yet they took the gospel to the entire Roman Empire in a single generation.

Why? How? They didn't have the financial resources we have. They did not have our state-of-the-art technology. A quill and scrap of parchment and some charcoal and oil-based ink was the zenith of their technological prowess. When they wrote a letter, instead of arriving at the speed of email, it could take weeks or months to arrive at its destination. In the absence of air travel or automobiles, their transportation was only as fast as a boat could sail, a horse could run, or a person could walk.

The small group, numbering about the size of a typical American congregation, possessed no money, no political connections, and no religious credentials. They operated with archaic transportation and communication options and only a handful of volunteers. Those deficiencies hardly seem to be a recipe for influencing the world. Even on a personal level, they certainly did not seem like a *special-ops unit* ready to change human history; but they did.

In spite of the early disciples' numerous initial shortcomings, they eventually had the one thing Jesus insisted they wait to receive before they moved a muscle: the power of the Holy Spirit.

The question before us is unavoidable: If Jesus's original disciples needed the power of the Holy Spirit, don't we?

Jesus and the Power of the Spirit

The four Gospels tell their stories of Jesus in a hurry in order to devote more detail to the last week of His life. In fact, more space is devoted to discussing the week leading up to His death than any other aspect of His story. So much attention is given to the Passion Week that one of the Gospels "has been called

7

little more than a passion account with a prologue."[3] The others are essentially the same.

The reason for bringing up the fact that approximately one-third of the entirety of the four Gospels describes only one week in the life of Jesus is to illustrate the way time is often compressed in the Gospel narratives. Weeks or even decades transpire between verses without a mention. The events are *telescoped* to draw attention to certain themes that are important to the conclusions the authors wished to emphasize. The compressing of time within the story results in other details being ignored without in anyway affecting the reliability of the message.

Telescoping clearly occurs in the final paragraphs of each Gospel. The writers are anxious to present a resurrected Jesus with accompanying final instructions to His chosen team. Consequently, we might be left with the impression that following the resurrection Jesus almost immediately ascended to heaven; but that is not the case.

Luke expands on the compressed details between the resurrection and the ascension in his second volume, the book of Acts. In the opening paragraph of the story about the origin of the early church, Luke gives his readers a glimpse of something we would not otherwise know, not even from his own telescoped timeline in his Gospel.

Jesus didn't ascend immediately after the resurrection. Instead, He spent more than a month instructing the disciples about how the Old Testament should be interpreted in light of a crucified and resurrected Savior. Luke describes it this way: "He presented himself alive to them after his suffering by many proofs, appearing to them during forty days and speaking about the kingdom of God" (Acts 1:3).

The Acts passage demonstrates that Jesus taught His disciples, on more than one occasion, they would be emissaries of a mission; and they would need the Holy Spirit's power to accomplish the task. It appears Jesus mentioned the need for the Holy Spirit's power at one of the earliest opportunities after the resurrection and at least once more just before the ascension (compare Luke 24:36-49 and Acts 1:1-11). No doubt Jesus taught them all about the Holy Spirit in the nearly six weeks between the resurrection and the ascension, and Luke provides us with a bookended report of His probable first, and likely last, lessons. We can assume there was much more we are not told. Let's look closely, therefore, at what Luke said about the power of the Spirit.

The Holy Spirit and the Word (Luke 24:44-49)

On the first Easter evening Jesus huddled with His closest followers to give them an early glimpse into their future. He told them He planned to give them a worldwide mission. That mission became the work of the early church, and it continues until the present. Their mission is our mission.

Can you imagine the shock and exhilaration the disciples must have been feeling at that moment? Luke makes the unusual observation, "They still disbelieved for joy" (v. 41). Maybe that's Luke's way of saying they were blown away! The vision of Jesus alive again was too much for their senses to handle. In spite of their initial response to the unprecedented miracle of the resurrection, their joy overloaded their doubt and fueled their emerging faith.

Jesus wasted no time. He wanted to talk about His vision for His church to evangelize the world; but how did Jesus unfold the layers of the vision He had for the church? What were the details? How did the promise of the Holy Spirit factor into that initial conversation?

The Message

When Jesus appeared, after the resurrection on that first Sunday night, He immediately reminded the first disciples that everything He had taught them had been an outgrowth of Scripture. He referred to it as "everything written about me in the Law of Moses and the Prophets and the Psalms" (v. 44). That description is a technical way of describing the three major divisions of the Hebrew Bible of Jesus's day. These divisions had a slightly different order and arrangement of books, but the same content of the thirty-nine books we call the Old Testament. Think about it. Who else in history would have the audacity to claim the entire Old Testament is actually about himself? Only Jesus has made that claim with integrity.

In addition, Jesus insisted the message of the church would be grounded in that same Scripture. Jesus affirmed unapologetically that the Old Testament predicts His life and His death on the cross. It becomes clear, after some consideration, Jesus intends for us to see His life and death as the unifying theme of the Old Testament and the core of the New Testament. Obviously, the New Testament had not been written; yet, within a few years, it joined the Old Testament as the message of the Jesus community—precisely as Jesus had predicted (John 14:26).

Luke, who gave us a mammoth contribution to the New Testament, was obviously intent on helping his readers recognize how the Old Testament predicts the ministry and message of Jesus. Luke's Gospel has Jesus repeating that detail in two separate incidents. For instance, earlier in chapter 24 the point is made concerning Jesus's relationship to the Old Testament in the familiar story of Jesus on the road to Emmaus (a resurrection story found nowhere else in the Bible). In that instance, Jesus highlighted the importance of understanding all of Scripture through the lens of His life and death (vv. 13-32). Luke tells us that Jesus, "beginning with Moses and all the Prophets . . . interpreted to them in all the Scriptures the things concerning himself" (v. 27). The disciples walking with Jesus to Emmaus described later how moved they were to hear the exposition of Jesus when they said, "Did not our hearts burn within us while he talked to us on the road, while he opened to us the Scriptures?" (v. 32).

In Luke's narrative, immediately after the encounter on the road to Emmaus, Jesus appeared to His more well-known disciples in Jerusalem and impressed upon them the same truth: the source of His message and, consequently, the church's message will be forever drawn from the Word of God. Luke crowds these stories back-to-back, so we cannot overlook the thrust of the Lord's mandate about Scripture.

While Jesus was addressing the disciples in Jerusalem, He did something both gracious and miraculous. He did for them what every succeeding generation and every disciple should pray He would do for us. Luke said it this way: "Then he opened their minds to understand the Scriptures" (v. 45). This was a moment of revelation. It was a moment of spiritual perception. Jewish men who had been raised on Scripture, who had spent at least three years with Jesus, needed spiritual illumination to comprehend the theme of God's Word. Jesus opened their minds so they could understand the Scripture. If we don't pause to ask Him to do the same for us we might be guilty of a sin of omission.

Jesus wants us to evangelize the world in the power of the Spirit.

We might reasonably assume the dawning of understanding was immediate and collective. All of a sudden they all "got it." Jesus pressed them to see that the death and resurrection of Jesus, along with preaching a message of repentance beginning at Jerusalem, had all been prophesied centuries earlier. Once they could understand the Scripture, they were ready to understand their mission. Jesus was direct: "You are witnesses of these things" (v. 48).

The word *witness* comes from the vocabulary of the courtroom. It meant then what it means now: a witness on a witness stand giving testimony to what he or she knows. We derive our English word *martyr* directly from the Greek word, since the early witnesses were willing to die for their testimony, thus giving the word its modern connotation.

So when Jesus said, "You are witnesses of these things," He meant more than just "You saw this." He also meant, "You're responsible now to tell about this." Jesus wants us to evangelize the world in the power of the Spirit.

At this point, most of us grasp the absolute necessity of an external power source to make the mission viable. We sense the immensity of the mission and the weakness of the missionaries. We sense it in ourselves. The message is powerful, but it is not all-powerful. For success we need the Word anointed by the Spirit. Jesus refused to send His followers into the world armed with the good news of His death and resurrection until they were "clothed with power from on high" (v. 49).

Jesus instructed His followers to pause before they reacted to the opportunity before them. Only the Holy Spirit could prepare them for what Jesus wanted them to do. Nothing has changed.

Jesus urged His disciples, who at that moment represented the entire church, to be "clothed with power from high." The Greek word for "clothed" is the source of our English word *endue* or *endow*. The endowment of the Holy Spirit is the prerequisite for all effective evangelism. This truth will be reemphasized in the last post-resurrection reference to the Holy Spirit's power, but in Luke's Gospel a significant truth was firmly established by the Lord Himself. The church needs the anointing of the Spirit upon the Word of God, or all of its evangelistic efforts are furious displays of impotence.

The Holy Spirit and Power (Acts 1:3-9)

I picture the day Jesus ascended into heaven as a beautiful, sunny day in Jerusalem. Given the time of year, that's probably a correct assumption. It was early summer when He ascended, after a forty-day training period with His closest team members.

In the first chapter of Acts we find a couple of references to the coming of the Spirit, which may be further examples of time compression. The first reference (vv. 4-5) seems to be a version of the same conversation found in the last chapter of Luke. We are reminded at the beginning of Acts that Jesus "presented himself alive to them after his suffering by many proofs, appearing to them during forty days and speaking about the kingdom of God" (v. 3). The next verses sound like, and probably are, a summary of what Luke described previously concerning the message from the first Easter Sunday. "And while staying with them he ordered them not to depart from Jerusalem, but to wait for the promise of the Father, which, he said, 'you heard from me; for John baptized with water, but you will be baptized with the Holy Spirit not many days from now'" (vv. 4-5). This is probably the first reference Jesus gave concerning the Holy Spirit immediately after the resurrection. It closely mirrors the instruction of Luke 24:49. Then, between verses 5 and 6, we should likely envision a gap of approximately forty days; so verses 6 through 8 are, most likely, the final words of Jesus on earth concerning the Spirit. These are the verses of interest to us at this point.

In the opening paragraphs of Acts, Luke allows us to eavesdrop on a conversation in which the disciples still seem blissfully ignorant about the global evangelistic mission of Jesus. They were more interested in politics than evangelism, inquiring with an almost unguarded exuberance about when Jesus might get around to setting up His kingdom in Jerusalem (v. 6). Fortunately, then as now, Jesus persistently and patiently walked His followers out of the shallow end of the pool of local, temporary political obsessions and into the deeper waters of His worldwide mission to evangelize the nations.

Clearly what Jesus wants for the entire church is better than temporary political gains. As citizens of earth we should want good governments; but the real mission of Jesus has to do with repentance, forgiveness, and salvation. Therefore, in response to overt political ambitions, Jesus counters with spiritual power. Instead of temporary kingdoms, He offers the kingdom of God. We think *right here, right now*, and Jesus seems to say, "Think bigger and further out." He wants His church to be filled with the power of the Holy Spirit, so He disregarded the disciples' small visions and promised them "power"—the kind they would need to reach "the end of the earth" (v. 8).

So when Jesus focused His little, infant church on the future, He always turned the conversation to the promise of the Holy Spirit. From the first Easter until the moments before His ascension forty days later, He drew their hearts toward the promise of power for witnessing around the world (Luke 24:49; Acts 1:8).

What lessons should we draw from Jesus's promises and instructions regarding a Spirit-filled church? For one thing, the most obvious reason Jesus wants to empower His church with the Spirit has to do with evangelism, witness, and missions to the world in our time. He never suggested we could evangelize in our own strength, ingenuity, denominational networks, or any other human effort. Jesus said we need to be Spirit-filled to win lost people to Christ.

The next observation is related. Jesus had a very small church, and He expected everyone among them to be evangelists filled with the Spirit. Today, especially in the West, we tend to individualize everything in Scripture as if it were written for us alone. The promise of the Holy Spirit's power for witness, however, is for the entire body of Christ, and there can be no exemptions. Jesus wants a massive, mobilized, Spirit-filled army of evangelistic followers to carry the gospel around the corner and around the world.

The Spirit-filled life is not reserved for some special category of *extreme-sports* believers, while the rest of us sit quietly and watch them do their thing. Soul winners are not just the *adrenaline-junkie* church members who bravely encounter strangers and dive into spiritual conversations, apparently unaware of the social distances most people respect. All of the pronouns in Acts 1:8 are plural: You *all* will receive power, you *all* will be his witnesses, and these things occur when the Holy Spirit comes upon you *all*.

The old saying that a chain is only as strong as its weakest link has been repeated often. Jesus rose from the dead with a mission for us, but we all need to be Spirit-filled in order to accomplish the mission. Imagine what would happen if your entire congregation began seeking the power of the Spirit in order to be more effective in evangelism. Now compare that breathtaking vision of an energized church to what we have at present. Isn't it time leaders called the churches back to being Spirit-filled, evangelistic, and passionate about reaching the lost?

If someone were to challenge everyone in the body of Christ to witness, what would need to change in your life? Well, Jesus is the *Someone* who has already challenged us to evangelize in the power of the Holy Spirit. The only thing we need now is Holy Spirit power.

Just after World War II, when Billy Graham was young and still with Youth For Christ, he was in England to preach. While there, he happened to hear Stephen Olford preach on the fullness of the Holy Spirit from Ephesians 5:18. Billy Graham was gripped with conviction and confided in Olford after the service that the message was for him, as he felt he needed the power of the Spirit on his own life.

It so happened that both men were scheduled next to be in Pontypridd in the south of Wales, so they agreed to meet. In Wales they fasted and prayed for two days, and Olford counseled Graham from Scripture on the fullness of the Spirit. Billy Graham was seated on the floor with his Bible open as they prayed, when suddenly he jumped to his feet exclaiming, "This is it! I've been filled! This will revolutionize my ministry."

The two agreed to meet again that night after Graham preached a youth service. Olford arrived late, but he knew something was different. He said it was as if the air was charged with electricity. The sports arena was packed with young people, and Billy Graham was preaching from the book of Daniel about the handwriting on the wall. Before he could even conclude his message, young people were pouring out of their seats and coming to the front to repent and turn to Christ. Nothing like it had ever happened before in a Billy Graham event.

Later that night, Dr. Olford spoke to his father about his new friend, Billy Graham, and said to his missionary father, "The world will hear from that young man." Of course, he was right. The entire world eventually heard Billy Graham. The power of the Holy Spirit had ignited his gifts in a powerful new way.[4]

The Holy Spirit doesn't promise to use all of us in the way He did Billy Graham, but God fills us with His Spirit so that all of us can be more effective in sharing the gospel. The Holy Spirit empowers the whole church to reach the whole world with the whole gospel! The power of the Spirit is the power to evangelize. A Spirit-empowered church will be an evangelistic church.

1 Christa Case Bryant, "Why Saddam Hussein Lied About Iraq's Weapons of Mass Destruction," *The Christian Science Monitor*, July 2, 2009, https://www.csmonitor.com/World/Global-News/2009/0702/why-saddam -hussein-lied-about-iraqs-weapons-of-mass-destruction.

2 Quoted from "Power and Authority," Lord Acton Quote Archive, Acton Institute, accessed January 9, 2019, https://acton.org/research/lord -acton-quote-archive.

3 Robert H. Gundry, *A Survey of the New Testament*, rev. ed. (Grand Rapids, MI: Zondervan, 1981), 77.

4 Dr. Stephen Olford personally shared this story with me, in even greater detail, over lunch in Fort Worth, Texas in 1986.

THE SPIRIT GIVES LIFE TO THE CHURCH

Acts 1–2

Ew life is exciting! That excitement usually expresses itself in a variety of ways. For instance, have you ever noticed how many baby pictures are posted on social media by new parents? New grandparents may be worse! Why shouldn't everyone be excited when a baby arrives? After all, a new baby in the family feels like a miracle.

In addition to the joy of parenting, new parents will also likely receive plenty of advice from experienced parents, whether they want it or not. So here's my unsolicited advice to young dads: If your pregnant wife wakes you up at 2:30 a.m. near her due date and says, "It's time," don't ask, "Are you sure?" Don't worry about how I know this is wrong—just trust me!

New parents will have a lot to learn, but loving their baby usually comes spontaneously. In fact, almost everybody loves babies, because new life is a miracle! The miracle of birth seems exciting, even when the infant being born is a new church.

A day came when the miracle of new life being celebrated was the church of Jesus Christ. The Holy Spirit brought the first church to life, and He continues to be the powerful source of life for the church today! The New Testament suggests no other source of life for the church.

Praying for New Life (1:12-14)

If we could emulate only one action from the days of the early church, it could surely be prayer. Prayer, as nothing else can, invites the Spirit to give life to the body of Christ.

On at least two separate occasions Jesus had promised the coming of the Spirit and prioritized a period of waiting as a precursor. In Luke 24:49 Jesus was emphatic, "And behold, I am sending the promise of my Father upon you. But stay in the city until you are clothed with power from on high."

Notice the word *stay*. In the original language it means to "cease all activity." Relevant to our understanding of this passage are two simple questions: How did the early followers interpret that instruction, and how might we?

Fortunately, we don't have to speculate about the early church's response because Luke tells us. The disciples divided their time between praise, worship, and prayer in the temple and pouring out their hearts in a nonstop prayer meeting in the upper room (Luke 24:53; Acts 1:14). For the ten days between the ascension and Pentecost, the disciples engaged in 24/7, night and day, worship and prayer.

As a result, the disciples entered into one of the most remarkable periods of congregational prayer ever imagined. In fact, one veteran minister examined the disciples' prayer meeting in the upper room and concluded that the early church didn't attend a prayer meeting—instead, the early church *was* a prayer meeting![1]

The birth of the church is a miracle of history, and the prayer meeting in the upper room was the delivery room where the miraculous labor occurred. Luke gives us insight into the upper room meeting, which directly helps us grasp the larger vision Jesus had for His church from the beginning. The disciples had been instructed by the Lord Himself to "stay in the city" as they waited on the outpouring of the Holy Spirit. It is the manner in which they waited that is so informative for us. They prayed; but not only did they pray, they devoted themselves to prayer (Acts 1:14).

The word *devoted* is a verb made up of two Greek words. The most literal translation sounds somewhat awkward in English. It would be something like "to endure toward." In other words, the idea conveyed shows us a congregation pressing forward or leaning in to prayer. The word *devoted* means they continued or, better yet, adhered to the action of prayer. It's a present tense verb, meaning it was continuous action. They never stopped praying. This habit of nonstop prayer marked the early church throughout the book of Acts.

All of this is a picture of something God planned ahead of time. Pentecost, as we will see, was a Jewish festival that for

Christians became the birthday of the church as we know it. God's plan for His church was that it would come to life and reproduce itself, preaching the message of salvation around the world into every generation. To do that, the "labor and delivery room" was a passionate congregational prayer meeting.

Simply put, the outpouring of the Spirit occurred at a prayer meeting. The pattern of prayer meetings, which give birth to movements, was established to produce life through the Spirit and the church. The rest of the book of Acts repeats this pattern numerous times. It challenges us to ask if the pattern of prayer that produces life is, in fact, what Jesus had in mind when He declared, "My house shall be called a house of prayer" (Mark 11:17).

As the disciples persisted in unceasing prayer, the days ticked on. We now know the prayer meeting lasted ten days—from ascension to Pentecost. The disciples were never told when the Spirit would be poured out, so they just kept praying. Their devotion is admirable, but there's more than human commitment happening in these passages. We are challenged to see the first disciples as our role models. They showed us how to create the culture of prayer where life can begin.

The desire to see a culture of prayer woven into our congregational life is on the hearts of a lot of Christians today. For instance, I was recently approached by a deacon who serves in a well-known Baptist megachurch. In his role as a leader, he wanted to acquire resources to help the deacons he leads to seek God in prayer. Clearly, today, there is a hunger for a fresh touch from God that is prevalent in many followers of Jesus.

As leaders, we know something is missing or, at least, underdeveloped in our experience. Christians around the world are asking if the pattern in the upper room is relevant and workable today. For many the answer is yes. The key for us is rebuilding the culture of prayer in which the early church was born, even though many of us are in busy churches with already packed calendars. We know a planned event about prayer would be wonderful, but leaders long for something even more. We need more than a "prayer conference" or another sermon on prayer. Instead, many of us are rethinking our typical approach to prayer and wondering how to move toward a real New Testament culture of prayer. As one of my friends says frequently, "We've seen what *we* can do. It's time to see what *God* can do."

Clearly the early church was determined to rely on prayer, and the rest of the book of Acts demonstrates irrefutably that prayer was more than merely a program or ministry of the church. Prayer was their culture. Prayer was their oxygen. Prayer created the environment where life could begin.

The urgent need of this moment is to recognize that Jesus has always intended to work through a praying church. The Spirit will always enliven the praying church. Life is a result of the Spirit's presence, and the Spirit is always present in a congregation where the atmosphere is saturated with prayer. The earliest disciples were devoted to prayer; and we should recognize their actions as a blueprint for church life today, in spite of the fact many churches fail to embrace the call of living in prayer. When we abandon the life-giving prayer meetings that invite the presence of the Spirit of God, we do so to our own detriment.

The other reproducible principle for creating an atmosphere of life revolves around the demographics in the upper room prayer meeting. In Acts 1:14 Luke reminds us, "All these with

one accord were devoting themselves to prayer, together with
the women and Mary the mother of Jesus, and his brothers."
The prayer meeting welcomed and involved female partici-
pants. Praying side by side with the apostles and Mary, Jesus's
mother, was a group identified only as "the women."

Inter-
cession
and praise
are gifts
everyone
can
exercise.

If you visit the Western Wall in Jerusalem, sometimes referred to colloquially as the Wailing Wall,
you will find people praying at all hours of the
day or night. It is probably the most well-known
place of prayer in the world. Conspicuously,
the men pray on one side, while the ladies
are praying on the other side of a small dividing fence. One might conclude that such
gender divisions were from ancient times;
but, in fact, the separation appears to be a
more recent development.[2] Regardless of the
political and theological rationale for having
the dividing fence at the Western Wall today,
such division was not a part of the early church's
prayer meeting in the upper room. Men and women
were all together in the prayer meeting, crying out to
God and begging for the outpouring of the Holy Spirit!

The Spirit breathed life into the church as a result of everyone's prayer. Intercession and praise are gifts everyone can
exercise; and when entire congregations join in unified prayer,
we can expect an avalanche of the Spirit's life-giving power in
our churches.

God is not waiting for us to merely read another book on
prayer or preach another sermon on prayer or attend another

conference on prayer. God is calling on us to unite in prayer! The life of the church depends upon it.

Remember, the ten-day prayer meeting was not an anomaly. Instead, it was God's foreordained plan to prepare for the birth of the church. It seems strange to us; but then again, little in our experience compares to three thousand passionate new believers joining our congregation in a single day. In other words, what we consider to be unusual efforts yielded unusual results.

Obviously, God didn't see ten days of prayer as unusual. Perhaps He watches from heaven, observing our prayer-starved congregations, and looks upon our shallow helplessness. He sees maybe the single greatest anomaly of all—a prayerless church.

Where does all of this leave us? Is the pattern of relentless congregational prayer a relic of our distant past? No. We are in a renaissance of rediscovering the power of the prayer meeting. Most of us have marveled at what God has done in churches that make prayer a priority. The Brooklyn Tabernacle in Brooklyn, New York is one leading example of a church that moved from being a struggling congregation to being a role model for churches around the world because they focused attention on their prayer meeting.[3]

Today there are more examples around the world of churches who have become prayer-focused, but the early church is our real model. What, then, can we take away from the upper room experience in order to see new life in our churches?

First, we must admit mission drift. The early church began in a long, passionate prayer meeting with the entire church in attendance. Today, however, if we have a prayer meeting at all, the attendance is low, and the meeting is jettisoned to a time and location with little expectation of success. In addition (let's be honest) the concept of a prayer meeting as we typically remember it isn't too appealing. Before you react as if I've said something strange, ask yourself how many people attended the last prayer meeting at your church as compared to the Sunday morning worship service. Let me ask this a different way: are we approaching the prayer meeting the right way? Are we undermining the chance of a successful prayer meeting by the way we plan the event?

Second, we must recommit ourselves to the priority of congregational prayer as the primary resource for preparing a spiritual environment. If we do, we will find new ways to design a prayer gathering that attracts and blesses our people. I am not talking merely about an attendance goal. I am advocating for finding ways to get our people back into passionate prayer meetings.

Finally, leaders must be prepared for at least two things as we reprioritize prayer: First, it will take time and effort to redirect the church toward the power of congregational prayer meetings, but it's worth it. Next, when God finally sends a breakthrough, the entire congregation can experience a sense of a sudden blessing, even though others have prayed faithfully in the past for months or years. The unmistakable presence of the Spirit changes everything, and nothing short of His presence will ever again be enough.

An Outburst of the Supernatural (2:1-5)

Are miracles even possible? Some people are confident they are not. For instance, Adam Gopnik, a writer for *The New Yorker* magazine stated with dogmatic certainty that no miracles have ever occurred, there is no heaven, and supernatural beings such as angels are pure fantasy.[4] Those kinds of assertions present a dilemma for Christians. The denial of the supernatural directly contradicts almost every page of our Bible. Nowhere is this is more true than in the origin story of the church in Acts. When we read the account of the supernatural power surge that birthed the church, we are left with few options. Either Luke got it wrong; miracles existed once but they don't anymore; or miracles still happen.

Luke in no way attempts to downplay the supernatural birth of the church; in fact, he insists on the opposite. He places the supernatural occurrences up front in the most conspicuous manner available to him as a writer. As a result of the Spirit's powerful arrival, the church, as we know it, was born. No birth announcement has ever been more spectacular.

Let's go back to the prayer meeting in the upper room to fully grasp the power of the Spirit's work. There were 120 disciples crowded into the large hall praying (1:15). It was a warm morning in late May, sometime before 9:00 a.m., and most, if not all, of the disciples were seated (vv. 2, 15). Just then, in that otherwise uneventful setting, everything changed forever.

After ten days of nonstop, day and night worship and prayer, "suddenly" the supernatural pierced the known with a breakthrough from the unknown. The church was "suddenly" born, even though there had been ten days of gestation in the womb of unceasing prayer. At least four miracles broke immediately into the experience of everyone in the upper room.

First, the disciples heard a strange sound. It was not wind or a noise from the street below. Instead, it was a miracle that closely resembled the sound of a hurricane, and it came from heaven. Notice the Bible does not say the wind blew. It says there came "from heaven a sound *like* a mighty rushing wind" (v. 2, italics mine). In other words, there was no rational source for the loud blast. It was a sound originating from the presence of God and manifesting itself supernaturally throughout the upper room. If God intended to get their attention, it worked.

Next, they saw something that still defies any simple description. Concurrent with the sound of a storm blowing through the room, fire appeared around the ceiling, divided into 120 individual flames about the size of a human tongue, and sought out each member of the prayer meeting the way a heat-seeking missile zeros in on its target. Then, the unexplainable flames "rested" on each of them. Imagine that for a moment. What would you think if a drop of flaming lava fell on your head from a ceiling engulfed in an inferno? If we think this scene was serene and placid, we have missed the obvious. It was arresting in its unsettling vibrancy. Hurricane force windstorms and fire dropping from the sky are frightening images to almost anyone on earth. Business as usual was officially over!

In one of the most understated sentences in the New Testament, Luke tells us: "And they were all filled with the Holy Spirit" (v. 4). Why is it understated? There are two reasons.

First, this sentence marks a new beginning in God's dealing with His people. In every previous instance when the Spirit appeared in order to "fill" a person, it was an individual, exclusive, limited event. One person, such as a prophet or the Lord Himself, was filled with the Spirit (1 Sam. 19:23-24; Luke 3:21). Scripture does not record an instance prior to Pentecost when an entire people group experienced the filling of the Holy Spirit all at once. God gives His church life in one way—through the outpouring of the Holy Spirit.

The second reason has to do with what happened next. Thousands of people were saved after only one sermon. Do you know how many conversions are recorded in Scripture between the resurrection and Pentecost, prior to the arrival of the Spirit? There were none. The power of the Spirit to accomplish the mission of the church is essential to the church's continued existence, and it cannot be overstated.

What does it mean to be filled with the Spirit? In a sense, this entire book you are reading deals with that subject. Here in Acts 2 we are exposed to the first encounter between the Spirit and the entire church. Is it safe to say the upper room is the blueprint for every infilling of the Spirit that follows for all the people of God? To be perfectly clear, the answer is yes *and* no. For one thing, even the book of Acts doesn't describe every encounter with the Spirit in exactly the same way we find detailed in Acts 2. No other sounds like tornadoes blowing through a room occur again, and neither do drops of fiery tongues.

On the other hand, there are similarities and promises we must take seriously. For instance, the outpouring of the Spirit is always viewed as a miraculous occurrence and is sometimes accompanied by other unusual circumstances. On one occasion the Spirit filled the church; and there were no sounds of wind, no fire, and no tongues. Instead, Peter and John and their friends experienced an earthquake (Acts 4:31). In any event, the infilling of the Spirit is intended to be represented as a supernatural experience, regardless of the occurrences surrounding it. Since the church is absolutely dependent upon the power of the Spirit for survival, the fact that every believer was filled with the Spirit is, in that way, a *blueprint* for the ongoing ministries of the church. What so clearly began as a direct result of the Spirit's power cannot be maintained in some other way while expecting similar results. God intends for His people to be Spirit-filled. The Holy Spirit gives life to the entire church.

In addition to the supernatural aspect of being filled with the Holy Spirit, we must not disregard the immersive quality of the experience. After all, in the predictions leading up to the outpouring at Pentecost, Jesus had used varied language to describe the filling of the Spirit; but all of those descriptions involve, for the believers, an all-encompassing experience. For instance, Jesus promised the disciples would be "clothed with power from on high" (Luke 24:49). Later, in Acts, He promised they would be "baptized with the Holy Spirit" (1:5). A few verses later, Jesus described what the Spirit would do at Pentecost as coming "upon" the disciples (v. 8).

The terminology, or vocabulary, has become important in doctrinal disputes around two of the terms, even though they seem to be used interchangeably in the description of the Spirit's arrival at Pentecost. For instance, Jesus predicted the disciples would be "baptized with the Holy Spirit," but in the next chapter Luke explains what happened using the phrase "filled with the Holy Spirit" (2:4). Solving the doctrinal differences that have piggybacked off of those two phrases is beyond the scope of this brief work; however, there is a unifying truth inherent in both. The thread of revelation running through all of the terminology concerning the arrival of the Holy Spirit points to the fact that the experience (baptized, filled, come upon, clothed, etc.) describes an all-enveloping experience.

Using the word "baptized," even as a metaphor, was an attractive way to predict what the church experienced at Pentecost, since it conjures the mental picture of the baptism in water practiced by the Jews, John the Baptist, Jesus, and His apostles. The phrase "baptized with the Spirit" would have triggered an expectation of an experience, which, like being immersed in the Jordan River, would be pervasive.

In addition to an immersive experience, the arrival of the Holy Spirit was transformative for the disciples and is further evidence of the life-giving nature of the Holy Spirit. The disciples were like different people after the coming of the Spirit. They were bold in their preaching, and they understood the Scripture and their role in the Kingdom as never before. They were energized in a way they could not have manufactured on their own, but their actions mimicked exactly what Jesus had predicted would happen. The Spirit's coming changed everything for all of the disciples. The church, as we know it, was born—actually came to life—as a result of Pentecost.

God intends for His people to be Spirit-filled.

The transformative power of God's Spirit is still essential in the lives of believers today. If our churches lack a sense of vitality, we need to ask these questions: Are the leaders teaching about God's Spirit? Are the people seeking life in the Spirit? This powerful new life was never intended for a few church leaders or some special faction of the church. The life of the Spirit was not intended only for a few denominations either. The life of the entire church is completely dependent upon the presence and fullness of the Holy Spirit for every believer.

Years ago I developed the habit of drinking club soda or sparkling water as a substitute for soft drinks. My love of club soda led my wife to buy me a machine to make club soda (carbonated water) at home. She gave it to me as a Christmas gift. It seemed to be the perfect gift, but there was one drawback. In order to make the sparkling water, we had to make it in a two liter bottle; that was the premeasured size allowed by the machine. The problem was, I never drank two liters at a time (that's a lot of water). So the rest would be left in the refrigerator, where my homemade sparkling water very quickly lost its *sparkle*; overnight the club soda went flat—it lost its fizz.

In a sense, the Christian life is designed to be like club soda compared to tap water. The Spirit brings a powerful blast of *sparkle* and life to an otherwise *flat* experience. Jesus never intended for any believer to live the Christian life apart from the fullness of the Holy Spirit. The life of the entire church, and the only possibility of lost people being supernaturally converted, is through the powerful life of the Holy Spirit!

Results of Spiritual Life (2:38-42)

In the power of the Spirit Peter stood and preached the first sermon of the church before thousands of Jewish pilgrims who were visiting Jerusalem for the Feast of Pentecost. It was a message full of passion and expertly articulated interpretations of multiple Old Testament passages. The first among those passages was an excerpt from Joel's prophecy regarding the outpouring of the Holy Spirit (2:16-21). Peter finally understood the age of the church had dawned in the upper room when he and the others had been filled with the Holy Spirit. He also understood that an Old Testament prophecy was being fulfilled, and from that time on the Holy Spirit would be poured out on "all flesh" (v. 17). In other words, the age of the Holy Spirit's work among people had now been fully realized. No longer would the Spirit rest on a few. Instead,

> Your sons and your daughters shall prophesy,
>   and your young men shall see visions,
>   and your old men shall dream dreams;
> even on my male servants and female servants
>   in those days I will pour out my Spirit, and
>   they shall prophesy." (vv. 17-18)

Following his explanation of the Spirit's ministry on the earth, Peter preached a convicting message about the crucifixion and resurrection of Jesus (vv. 22-36). As a result, thousands of people immediately repented and placed their faith in Christ. Peter explained to them they would "receive the gift of the Holy Spirit" in addition to the forgiveness of their sins (v. 38).

Every believer is brought to life in conversion by the power of the Holy Spirit. Later, Paul would reinforce this teaching when he wrote, "No one can say 'Jesus is Lord' except in the Holy Spirit" (1 Cor. 12:3). The Holy Spirit gives life to the entire church. No one who is a follower of Jesus can be born again apart from the power of the Spirit.

Recently I read a strange report regarding the nearly twelve thousand Americans who have accidentally been declared dead by the United States government, due to keystroke errors at the Social Security Administration. Can you imagine how difficult your life would be if you had to prove you weren't dead? You couldn't get a bank loan, a driver's license, or social security payments for retirees; and the list of oddities grows from there. The article made one statement that particularly caught my attention: "Being dead makes it very hard to do the things needed to live."[5] How true!

That weird story reminds me of this biblical truth: the Spirit of God has come to breathe life into the entire body of Christ; and until that occurs, a dead church cannot do what a live church can. We need the Holy Spirit to live!

1 Armin R. Gesswine, *With One Accord in One Place: The Role of Prayer in the Early Church* (Terre Haute, IN: Prayer Shop Publishing, 1998), 13.

2 Amanda Borschel-Dan, "When Men and Women Prayed Together at the Western Wall," *The Times of Israel*, June 29, 2017, https://www.timesofisrael.com/when-men-and-women-prayed-together-at-the-western-wall.

3 Jim Cymbala, *Fresh Wind, Fresh Fire: What Happens When God's Spirit Invades the Hearts of His People* (Grand Rapids, MI: Zondervan, 1997), 23-38.

4 Adam Gopnik, "Bigger than Phil," *The New Yorker*, February 17 & 24 issue, https://www.newyorker.com/magazine/2014/02/17/bigger-phil.

5 Marissa Fessenden, "About 12,200 People Are Erroneously Declared Dead Every Year by the U.S. Government," Smithonian.com, June 10, 2015, https://www.smithsonianmag.com/smart-news/about-12200-people-are-erroneously-declared-dead-every-year-us-government-180955549.

3

THE SPIRIT ENCOURAGES THE CHURCH

Acts 4:1-31

Y ou've probably heard the cynical old saying, "No good deed goes unpunished." Unfortunately, even when we hate to admit it, in some instances the old saying seems true.

For example, the early church experienced persecution and resistance even when they were doing exactly what they were called to do. Their response to injustice, however, was a blueprint for dependence upon the Holy Spirit's ministry. As a result, in numerous ways, those first believers serve as excellent role models for a Spirit-led ministry today. How they responded to discouragement presents us with a lighted pathway forward through the potential setbacks and roadblocks we inevitably face in our lives.

Discouragement due to injustice and harsh circumstances seems to be universal. Christians are not exempt. For instance, a friend of mine was raised in Eastern Europe during the days of Communism and was regularly persecuted for his faith in Christ. Yet, in spite of the brutality orchestrated against him, he refused to stop preaching and teaching about Jesus. So, when he was still a young man, he was arrested and tortured for no reason other than being an outspoken believer in that hostile country. The authorities didn't break his spirit or his faith, but they used inhuman treatment and physical abuse as a systematic strategy to discourage him and others like him.

We may think of discouragement as an emotional issue, and it often is; but discouragement frequently emerges in the form of actions taken by those in authority to suppress any expression of our faith. Of course, we might think of current persecution in places such as North Korea, Syria, or Iran, since the Christian faith is brutally attacked in those places.[1] We have abundant evidence pointing to the fact that hostility to the gospel is spreading in our times. Unfortunately, the intense persecution of Christians, used as a strategy for discouraging the body of Christ, is nothing new. It began almost as soon as the first believers were empowered at Pentecost! But the Holy Spirit is still alive and well, encouraging the discouraged church.

The Strategy of Discouragement

While we don't have access to an exact timeline from the exciting days of the early church, it seems from the text as if only a short time had passed after Pentecost when the hostile religious leaders in Jerusalem launched a strategic attack designed to discourage the rapidly growing Jesus movement in the Holy City. The miracles among God's people were frequent and undeniable (v. 16). Those miracles in the rapidly growing church were an affront to the religious establishment, and personal jealousies drove the hatred leveled toward the followers of Jesus.

For instance, one afternoon when Peter and John, the clear leaders of the swelling Jesus movement, were walking to the temple for prayer, a beggar sitting near the Beautiful Gate on the eastern side of the temple asked them for financial assistance. The man was obviously disabled from a congenital deformity in his legs. Peter, who had no money, countered instead with an offer of hope in the name of Jesus; and the man was saved and healed (3:1-8).

The miracle in a busy public area near the temple infuriated the religious leaders. From their perspective, something had to be done. These same religious leaders had plotted the crucifixion of Jesus a few months earlier, expecting death to end His influence, but the opposite had occurred. The Jesus movement was growing, and now the followers of Jesus were performing miracles just as He had done.

Since the miracle of the man born with crippling disabilities had occurred in a busy high-traffic area, and since the healed man's response had been so dramatic, uninhibited, and celebratory, the incident attracted a crowd of curious onlookers. Today we would say the whole incident went viral. Peter seized the opportunity to preach to the gathering crowd.

While the formerly crippled man was running wildly, praising God joyfully and showing his gratitude to Peter and John by pausing occasionally to hug them enthusiastically, Peter told the crowd about Jesus. We might assume the crowd that gathered to hear Peter was fairly large, since Luke adds the detail that they were in Solomon's portico, an expansive area on the perimeter of the temple grounds (v. 11-26). It was an area capable of accommodating thousands of people.

The crowd size in the temple area alerted the priests to the growing threat of the Jesus follow-ers, so they had Peter and John arrested im-mediately (4:1-2). Peter and John remained in custody overnight; and the next day, behind closed doors, the strategy of forceful intim-idation and threats began.

Christians are not exempt from discourage-ment.

Imagine the scene: Peter and John had lived their entire lives in small fishing vil-lages in northern Israel, far removed from the political theater common among the powerful priest class who collaborated regularly with the Roman Empire. The priests were, in a manner of speaking, Jewish nobility. They controlled the day-to-day operations of the temple where common Galilean working-class Jews like Peter and John had come their entire lives once or twice a year to worship the God of their ancestors. The priests were a fraction of the population, but they were venerated by the people of Israel. They were God's chosen representatives and servants and had descended from Moses's brother, Aaron. Their pedigree was highly respected.

The probability of intimidation was virtually guaranteed when common people were in the presence of their religious leaders. The scene presented by Luke's expert retelling of the event couldn't be written more precisely. He deftly recreates the heavy and oppressive ambiance of the all-too-common image of power crushing weakness. Imagine this event and how you might feel: "On the next day their rulers and elders and scribes gathered together in Jerusalem, with Annas the high priest and Caiaphas and John and Alexander, and all who were of the high-priestly family. And when they had set them in the midst, they inquired, 'By what power or by what name did you do this?'" (vv. 5-7).

The apostles had been cooling their heels overnight in jail, and the next day a virtual *Who's Who* of the religious ruling class surrounded them like wild dogs circling wounded prey. The full-court press of strategic intimidation and discouragement was initiated. The powerful religious aristocracy wanted the Jesus movement to end, so they pulled out all the stops.

I have been in a few meetings where men, convinced of their own spiritual superiority, gathered to undermine their opponents. In my experience, there are few things more egregious or more clearly un-Christlike than powerful men and women using religious zeal to justify or maintain their last gasps of power and control. Unfortunately, no matter how sickening it appears, it frequently works. The often frail, outnumbered church of Jesus never needed the Holy Spirit to come through more than at times of discouragement and intimidation when raw, unbridled worldly power masqueraded as God's will.

The Unexpected Encouragement of the Spirit (vv. 1-22)

Anyone who might have seen the two uneducated fishermen surrounded by the intimidating, powerful ruling class of elite

39

religious leaders would have concluded the fishermen were hope-lessly outnumbered and in over their heads. The strategy of dis-couragement was on full display, but the fishermen were armed with something the religious heavyweights failed to appreciate. The Holy Spirit delights in giving courage when His people have been discouraged.

Immediately, as the interrogation began, Peter surprised the interrogators by asserting himself with a bold confidence he had noticeably lacked the night Jesus was betrayed. Luke leaves nothing to speculation about the reason for the dramatic change in the apostle. "Then Peter, filled with the Holy Spirit, said to them, 'Rulers of the people and elders'" (v. 8). Sud-denly Peter was direct, confident, and willing to confront the discouragement being layered on his team. Why? The answer is clear: the Holy Spirit encourages His people in the face of discouragement. The Spirit lifts the fallen and can reverse the old established order of power dominating apparent weakness. If that weren't the case, the church of Jesus would have died in its infancy.

The response to Peter's unexpected boldness was priceless. "Now when they saw the boldness of Peter and John, and per-ceived that they were uneducated, common men, they were as-tonished. And they recognized that they had been with Jesus. But seeing the man who was healed standing beside them, they had nothing to say in opposition" (vv. 13-14). The Holy Spirit was the game changer in that situation, and the Spirit-filled apostles astonished the critics. Jerusalem's religious elite were struck with three unassailable realities: First, the apostles were not humanly equipped to speak with such convincing authority.

Second, the man who had been healed was present for the trial, and he was still in excellent health. Finally, the Spirit-filled apostles reminded the religious leaders of Jesus! The critics were left without an adequate response. All they could muster were some hollow threats aimed at discouraging the apostles from serving the Lord; but their discouraging threats fell flat.

Through the numerous stories Luke wrote, he communicated a theme for the church of the future. The chapters of Acts, filled with one story after another, are not random, haphazard, unrelated vignettes. They are a collection of carefully researched events tied together to tell a bigger story. So what is Luke's story? Plainly, Acts is a picture of how God wants His church to operate, thrive, and live. The unifying thread through the tapestry of Luke's narrative is the ongoing ministry of the Holy Spirit.

When persecution and trouble developed, the Holy Spirit was there to shift the balance of power and change otherwise predictable outcomes. The early church didn't have greater strength or resolve or talent than we have today. These believers merely learned early to depend upon the Holy Spirit.

Take notice of exactly how the Holy Spirit helped the apostles while they were on trial, as it is important. The discouraging circumstances weren't miraculously changed. The accusers who were spewing their discouraging threats weren't suddenly racked with guilt or miraculously converted. Instead, those who were being systematically discouraged were filled with the Holy Spirit and fresh encouragement. The apostles weren't rescued from the problem; they were filled with spiritual power to face the discouragement and the attacks.

What attacks have you experienced? How have you been discouraged? The same Holy Spirit who filled the apostles can fill you. The encouragement in the face of discouragement they received from the Spirit is available to you too. Are you discouraged about your family? Do you feel overwhelmed financially? Have you received alarming news from the doctor? Even if the trouble remains, God's Spirit can fill you with the encouragement you need to keep going in faith and not give up!

The Holy Spirit encourages His people in the face of discouragement.

In my own life the Holy Spirit has been a constant source of encouragement. As a teenager, far from God, I rarely applied myself at school. In fact, I didn't graduate from high school. My life was careless, undisciplined, and rebellious. Then one night, miraculously, under a sudden and surprising conviction, I surrendered my life to Christ. Within a month, through an unexpected set of circumstances, I was a college student without a high school diploma thousands of miles away from home. I wanted to live for Christ, but it was difficult. I was lonely, trying to become a student after years of academic apathy, and attempting to live the Christian life with virtually no knowledge of the Holy Spirit.

I was working on my prayer life, reading the Bible for the first time, joining street evangelism teams, and struggling to stay caught up in the new academic demands thrust upon a university student. Most of the time, I felt as if I was pushing a rock uphill and making little progress. I was determined to live for Christ, but I did not know how to rely upon the Holy Spirit. Still, I was reading the Bible, attending prayer meetings, and growing more aware of the promise of the Holy Spirit. I was grateful to be a follower of Christ, and I never wanted to turn away from Him; but I recognized there was a big difference between what I read in the book of Acts and my experience. When I reached out to a pastor to learn more about the Holy Spirit, he discouraged me and warned, "Be careful with that!" Not only were my circumstances discouraging, I was discouraged verbally from learning about or pursuing the help of the Holy Spirit. Fortunately, God is never discouraged. He had something more in store for me. One quiet night, alone in my dorm room, I knelt beside my bed and prayed God would fill me with His Spirit. That night God heard my prayer; I was filled with the Spirit, and my Christian life has never been the same. While my personal experience isn't a model for everyone, I mention it here to insist you do not have to live in discouragement or dissatisfaction in your Christian life. You do not have to allow anyone to discourage you in the Lord's work when the Holy Spirit is so immediately available to you.

The Entire Church Encouraged (vv. 23-31)

If the story of the apostles on trial had ended with their release, it would still stand as a powerful example of the Spirit's power; but the story does not end there. What happened next is a vital key to understanding the ministry of the Holy Spirit to the entire body of Christ.

The two apostles hurried back to the home base of Christian operations in Jerusalem to give the church an update. The entire church needed to be aware of the circumstances that had transpired since the apostles had been publicly arrested the day before. No doubt the church knew of the apostles' detainment, since it happened in the middle of the day in front of hundreds, or perhaps thousands, of witnesses. We can safely assume an incredible prayer meeting was taking place while the leaders of the church were incarcerated. Prayer was their natural response to everything. No wonder Peter and John knew exactly where to go to find their people. They headed to the place of prayer!

Once they rejoined with the church, the apostles reported what the religious leaders had said. They recounted the miracle, the arrest, and the harsh warnings not to teach in the name of Jesus.

Imagine what the new believers must have been thinking and feeling. A few months earlier, those religious leaders and priests had arranged to have the Messiah crucified. Now the same people—the highest ranking officials of the religion, including the high priest and his family—had arrested the apostles and threatened them to never mention Jesus again. The strategy of discouragement had reached a new level of intensity.

When the new Christians heard the discouraging news, some of them must have been defiant. Others probably were worried about their families, their futures, and their lives. After all, the early church was made up of Jewish converts who had only recently begun following Jesus. They were only beginning to learn about the new way of life in Christ. In addition, they had grown up respecting and, in some cases, fearing the priests and Jewish religious leaders. How would these new converts respond to this discouraging report from the religious authorities conveyed by the apostles?

Prayer Changes Things

In the book of Acts there is a dynamic relationship between prayer and the Holy Spirit. This event recorded in Acts 4 is one of the best examples of that close connection. When the apostles informed the young church that the priests discouraged them from preaching in Jesus's name, the response was immediate. The entire church began to cry out in passionate prayer! They may not have known it when they started to pray, but the Holy Spirit was about to send shockwaves through their faith in answer to their prayer.

The prayer of these believers was filled with faith, even in the midst of their drastic circumstances. Yes, the highest-ranking leaders of their ancestral religion had discouraged them from mentioning Jesus again; but, through prayer, they bypassed the authority of men and appealed directly to the authority of heaven! Their first words in prayer reveal their faith in a big God who can handle easily His people's moments of discouragement: "And when they heard it, they lifted their voices together to God and said, 'Sovereign Lord, who made the heaven and the earth and the sea and everything in them'" (v. 24).

The religious rulers were intimidating, but in prayer the church called on a power far more impressive, larger, and higher ranking in authority. Instead of cowering before the discouragement of the religious dignitaries, the church appealed to the "Sovereign Lord." Our spiritual ancestors knew how to pray things into a proper perspective!

The new believers also turned to Scripture to feed their prayer and fuel their faith. Recalling King David's prophecy that the Gentiles would "rage," the people would "plot in vain," and the rulers would gather together "against the Lord and against his Anointed," they saw their own situation (vv. 25-26). They recognized the persecution and discouragement they were experiencing was actually part of God's larger plan for their lives. They prayed, "For truly in this city there were gathered together against your holy servant Jesus, whom you anointed, both Herod and Pontius Pilate, along with the Gentiles and the peoples of Israel, to do whatever your hand and your plan had predestined to take place" (vv. 27-28).

The prayers of the church were, as virtually every other prayer recorded in Acts with limited exceptions, reflective of a group in prayer. In other words, the whole church prayed. They had discovered the truth that prayer meetings change the world. They were desperate. There is obvious desperation inherent in their words, "Why did the Gentiles rage?" Still, they were confident and filled with faith, because they recognized God's hand in the events of history—even those events that were painful for a season. In spite of the discouraging threats leveled against them, their faith pressed on; and they asked God to give them boldness in the face of threats and discouragement. They expected the threats to continue, so they prayed for more miracles to occur in order to counter the discouragement from the priests (vv. 29-30).

Can you imagine that kind of faith and how our world could be changed if more of us faced discouragement by asking God to give us the opportunity to *double down* on our preaching and ministry? If more of our church members joined prayer groups to cry out for miraculous salvations and healings, how would that kind of faith affect our cities? How would boldness from our pastors and street evangelism teams affect the lostness of our neighborhoods? How would passionate, congregational prayer change the spiritual climate of our own churches? I ask simply: If we did what they did, what might happen?

Perhaps the most powerful answer to a hypothetical question is a review of what actually did happen in response to the desperate, but courageous, prayer of the threatened early church. As they were praying, something reminiscent of Pentecost occurred. "And when they had prayed, the place in which they were gathered together was shaken, and they were all filled with the Holy Spirit and continued to speak the word of God with boldness" (v. 31).

> There is a dynamic relationship between prayer and the Holy Spirit.

Before delving into the miracle of the Holy Spirit's activity in response to their prayer, we should briefly take one last look at the prayer itself. In this instance, Luke uses a word that isn't rare, but it is not the most common word for prayer in the New Testament. It is a word that reflects the need and desperate nature of this prayer, because it springs from the root word meaning "to lack"; and, therefore, is sometimes used to mean "beg." The use of this word by Luke (one of the two most-sophisticated Greek linguists among the New Testament authors) indicates the seriousness and urgency of this prayer. The believers knew that the priests who threatened and discouraged them had the power to harass them, incarcerate them, or worse. They knew they had no power within themselves. They were praying from a position of great need.

Is it possible to so misunderstand or overestimate ourselves when we approach God in prayer that we miss completely God's best? Do our denominational ties or our networks or our past achievements occasionally create a false sense of strength and self-reliance? It has happened before. Remember the parable Jesus told of the Pharisee who bragged to God about his spiritual accomplishments and disdained the sinful tax collector? Jesus said the self-confident Pharisee left the prayer meeting without connecting to heaven at all. Why? He was too *strong* in himself. He wasn't needy. He was a failure in prayer due to his own assessments of his successes elsewhere (Luke 18:9-14). Jim Cymbala focused on this particular aspect about prayer in a succinct observation. "God is attracted to weakness."[2]

The threatened disciples in Jerusalem knew the circumstances in which they found themselves were desperate, and desperate prayer pulls at God's heart. When we become desperate enough to believe prayer is our only way forward, we will see God move in our marriages, churches, cities, and beyond.

The Holy Spirit Encourages

As the early believers were praying, the Holy Spirit *rocked their world* with an earthquake! Three distinct developments actually occurred at that prayer meeting that signaled God's approval in answer to their prayers. For one thing, "the place . . . was shaken." The word *shaken* in the Greek New Testament describes the powerful surge of ocean waves during a storm at sea. It carries with it the idea of "unsettling a thing." Isn't that just like God? In answer to prayer about an unsettling discouragement, He sent an unsettling tremor that felt similar to being on the deck of a ship during a typhoon. It's as if God was saying, "Don't worry about the shaky culture you live in—I'm going to shake things up even more!"

The next event that revealed the presence of God involved the powerful awareness that everyone in the prayer meeting was being filled with the Spirit in a fresh wave of outpouring. This passage reminds us the Holy Spirit can fill us repeatedly, since some in this group had been filled with the Holy Spirit a few weeks earlier at Pentecost.

In the New Testament, only Luke uses this particular word to describe the fullness of the Holy Spirit. In other places, the Greek word for "filled" describes a wedding party filled with guests (Matt. 22:10), a sponge filled with liquid (Matt. 27:48), or an expectant mother whose pregnancy has reached full term (Luke 2:6). In other words, to be filled with the Spirit means you are filled to capacity!

When my son was in college and needed gas in his car, whenever I would pay for it he would fill the tank so full the gas was visible at the opening of the tank. That's called *topping it off.* When the tank is "topped off" it has reached its capacity— it can't hold another drop. That's what God wants to do in our lives. He wants to fill our lives so full of the Spirit that we reach maximum capacity. Pray right now that God would fill you to capacity. God wants to fill everyone in His church.

Finally, the believers "continued to speak the word of God with boldness." The strategy of discouragement didn't work against this Spirit-filled church! The entire church was filled with the Spirit and overflowing with courage. The encouragement of the Holy Spirit is a ministry to the entire body of Christ, not just to a few.

Does all of this tell us anything about how to process discouragement? Spirit-filled believers who are willing to pour their lives out for Jesus will naturally face numerous challenges and unrelenting pressures; but the Spirit will encourage them by filling them and using them for His purposes.

One day a friend of mine showed me a photo he had taken many years earlier of a plaque in front of a now closed, tiny church in the middle part of the state of Georgia. The plaque in the picture told the story of an unusual prayer. In 1886 the Red Level Methodist Episcopal Church was declining. One Sunday the preacher was thundering a sermon about the end of the world and judgment day. A massive and deadly earthquake had recently occurred in Charleston, South Carolina, and word of its destruction had reached the attention of people throughout the South. So, as part of his sermon that day, the pastor decided to pray for an earthquake to strike his church if it would bring sinners to repentance. Immediately, as he prayed that odd prayer, an earthquake rocked the little wooden church and the congregation fled the building. After the earthquake that morning, when the congregation went back inside, they listened to their preacher more carefully than before!

Truthfully, we shouldn't expect an earthquake every time we pray or every time the Holy Spirit encourages us when we are discouraged. What we *can* expect is the Holy Spirit to show up in power when we need His comfort and reassurance most. He may not shake the earth, but His presence can shake us up from the inside out and encourage us to stand strong in the face of discouragement. He's done it before, and He will do it again—for you!

4

THE SPIRIT MOBILIZES THE CHURCH

Acts 8; 11:19-26; 13:1-4

Do you like Ferris wheels? Actually, I can easily imagine someone saying, "Are you kidding me?" After all, even the mention of a Ferris wheel may conjure a quaint, old-fashioned memory of a low-grade thrill from another, and slower, generation. But not all of them belong in a black and white movie from the '50s.

For instance, what would you think about twenty-five dollars per person to ride a kind of *next generation* Ferris wheel that rises more than four hundred feet above ground, while you and more than a dozen others get a sweeping view of the city below from almost any angle? The Orlando Eye in Orlando, Florida is like few Ferris wheels ever imagined. For one thing, instead of sitting in an open, exposed bucket seat, the Orlando

Eye allows you to sit or stand in a large glass cube—like a small, clear room—where fifteen or so other people are either standing or sitting. Music and announcements are piped in. It's air-conditioned, and the view is astounding.

It sounds incredible, doesn't it? Except one day in July 2015 something went wrong. There was a power outage, and the Orlando Eye stalled. The people in the top cube were left suspended in a glass room four hundred feet above the ground. They couldn't be reassured either, because when the power went out the sound system stopped working. Then there was the issue of the air conditioning. It stopped too. It was July and the hottest part of the day in Central Florida. So, fifteen passengers per cube were trapped in a suspended *greenhouse,* baking in the Sunshine State's famous, irrepressible sun with nowhere to escape the intense heat. They were stuck there for two long, brutal hours. And, one other thing, there was obviously no bathroom. Take a moment and let this scenario sink in. It was terrible.

Fortunately, after more than two hours, the power was restored; and the people were eventually back on the ground, where they received immediate medical attention. No one was seriously affected due to the mishap.[1]

Why do I mention the story of the Orlando Eye power outage? It feels frustrating every time I think about it, because I imagine myself or my family—if we were stuck—as so many other people were. Could there be anything more frustrating than being absolutely immobile when you're supposed to be moving?

I live in Austin, Texas, one of the fastest growing cities in the country, with a net increase of more than fifty new cars on our highways and roads every single day of the year. Sometimes

I wonder if they are all headed the same direction I'm going! Austin has been identified as one of the most congested cities in America. Everyone feels it. At the end of a workday, when I am headed home, I join the migration of cars creeping along at a snail's pace. For many miles I average between two and five miles per hour, with occasional bursts of ten to twenty miles per hour. I have tried shortcuts, of course, only to learn the hard way that hundreds of other commuters have thought of the same alternatives. No matter where we drive in Austin, we move slowly, if we move at all. There is something mind numbing about wanting to break free and go, when you are stuck in traffic as far as the eye can see.

Think about it. Human beings are built for movement. We don't like being stuck in a swinging, elevated glass cube or a traffic jam. From the time a baby is born, she is unconsciously wired to squirm and kick and crawl; until, one day, she learns the independence of walking. We are made to move, and we don't do well when we are trapped in gridlock.

Similarly, the Holy Spirit built the church for action and movement and mission. When the church slows down and becomes immobile, she becomes ineffective and no longer resembles her calling; and she gets frustrated. The Holy Spirit has called us to mobilize. But, sometimes, even those who know they should be on the move don't move much at all.

The Church That Wouldn't Move (ch. 8)

For those who know a little about the story of the early church, you might remember Jesus rose from the dead and instructed His church to get going! He promised the Holy Spirit to help propel the fishermen, tax collectors, and the other disciples into a worldwide mission of global evangelization (1:8). When we read about that day, we would assume they were ready to ship off to distant lands immediately; but it didn't happen that way.

God blessed the church in Jerusalem, and they were overcoming their growing pains. They must have been fairly comfortable in Jerusalem, because quite a bit of time had passed—a few years at least—since Pentecost, and the church was still a Jewish-centric movement headquartered in Jerusalem. A few Gentiles had come to Christ but nothing to the extent Jesus had promised. The church was content and getting sedentary, even though they were experiencing blessings. But their lethargy about reaching the nations was about to change.

God always finds a way to mobilize His church.

Political unrest in Rome, which had nothing to do with the church at first, and religious tensions in Jerusalem were brewing into a dangerous, explosive cocktail that was about to blow up in the face of the "Jesus" community. The tipping point came when Stephen the deacon was murdered outside the city walls of Jerusalem. The Jewish religious leaders were energized by the execution of Stephen. "And there arose on that day a great persecution against the church in Jerusalem, and they were all scattered throughout the regions of Judea and Samaria, except the apostles" (8:1). It was a terrible ordeal for our brothers and sisters in the early church because they were expelled from their homes and families. Yet God used the deportation of thousands of believers from Jerusalem to begin the worldwide spread of the message of new life in Christ to the Roman Empire. They reached their western world in a single generation.

The church had not responded to the missionary heart of God in a timely manner, so the persecution that expelled the Christians actually helped to accomplish the Great Commission of Jesus. In spite of the pain and suffering they must have experienced, unleashing thousands of Spirit-filled Jesus followers on the cities in and around Israel had the exact opposite effect the Jewish leaders had envisioned. The exiled church became an evangelistic refugee movement, almost against its collective will.

God gets things done. Through His Spirit He always finds a way to mobilize His church—sometimes even when they don't want to move!

The Antioch Awakening

Antioch was an important center of the burgeoning, worldwide Jesus movement, and it was in the middle of a spiritual awakening. Somehow, I think most of us underestimate this portion of the Christian story in the book of Acts. What was happening in Antioch was amazing. Luke devoted a lot of space in his narrative to the characters and the drama unfolding in Antioch. What happened there shifted the world's future. Because of the Spirit's direct intervention, Europe would hear the gospel; and the Roman Empire would be flooded with the story of Jesus, the Jewish Messiah. After Antioch, Jesus would be seen as the Savior of the entire world; and the Jewish-centric boundaries on the message of the church would be altered forever. The Antioch awakening and the leaders' prayer summit that occurred there was one of the most decisive victories of the Holy Spirit since Pentecost. Every non-Jewish believer today should feel a kinship to Antioch. We are here, in part, because of what the Spirit did there.

In the days of the early church, Antioch was known as *Syrian Antioch*, about five hundred miles northwest of Jerusalem. Due to changes in international borders over the centuries, however, today it is surrounded by the modern city of Antakya in south central Turkey.

During the days of the early church expansion, Antioch was a big city; in fact, it was the third largest city in the Roman Empire, with a population of an estimated five hundred thousand people.²

Antioch was one of the beneficiaries of the deportation of Christians from Jerusalem. Since the city of Antioch already had a thriving Greek-speaking Jewish business community, and since the early Christians were all Jewish, Antioch was a preferred destination for the exiled believers.

Once they were in the city, the believers started evangelizing and winning people to Christ. In fact, so many new believers were coming to Christ in Antioch, the apostles got word of the spiritual awakening taking place. Barnabas, an early leader and close friend of the apostles, was sent from Jerusalem to investigate the reports about the fresh moving of the Spirit in Antioch. When Barnabas arrived, the movement of people coming to Christ only increased. The Spirit was clearly moving in the city.

Antioch serves as a blueprint of sorts, because it was the first city in biblical history to evangelize itself without any input from the original apostles. That's how we do it today, of course; but prior to Antioch, it had never occurred. The Jesus movement was picking up momentum, and things were changing in ways no one but God could have foreseen. What would happen next changed the world.

Saul of Tarsus Goes to Antioch (11:19-26)

When Barnabas saw the powerful swell of new believers coming to Christ, he knew he needed help. Fortunately, he knew a young believer who had come to Christ a few years earlier who had unusually powerful spiritual gifts. For one thing, the young Jewish convert had an unprecedented discipline about his spiritual life. He had mysteriously spent three years, essentially alone, in the Arabian Desert, seeking solitude and fellowship with God as a way of growing closer to Jesus. When he returned, his preaching and teaching gifts, his prayer life, his insight into the gospel, his intellect, his testimony, and his zeal were unrivaled. The Holy Spirit was clearly upon him.

Knowing this, the rugged trip that would be needed in order to find him was justified. So Barnabas left the spiritual awakening and went across the mountain range to the commercially prosperous city of Tarsus (located today in south central Turkey) to find the brilliant young believer. Once he found him, Barnabas convinced him to leave his tent-making career; and he brought Saul of Tarsus to Antioch (vv. 25-26).

For one year the young, Bible-teaching Saul explained Scripture and discipled the new believers. The new converts were so passionate about their faith that it wasn't long before their unusual fervor—stirred in part by their new teacher, Saul of

Tarsus—earned them a nickname: "And in Antioch the disciples were first called Christians" (v. 26). Saul was making a mark for the kingdom of God.

When the Spirit Moves a Church (13:1-4)

After Saul had been in Antioch for a year, so many people had become followers of Christ that the city became a role model of what the Spirit can do to change the spiritual climate of an entire city. Scores of people had been saved and discipled. It was a city experiencing revival.

What an incredible time to be involved in ministry! Like revivals in our history—the Welsh Revival of 1904–1905, the Hebrides Revival of 1949, or the Jesus movement of the late 1960s and early 1970s—not only did the awakening change the new converts, the revival changed the leaders too. No preacher or Bible teacher could come of age in a spiritual awakening and ever be the same or be satisfied with less.

Perhaps the leaders of the movement were at a crossroads about what to do next. God had obviously done something significant, but what did He want them to do going forward? Did they begin to sense the Spirit calling them in a new direction? I believe that's what they were considering when the leaders of the city movement retreated into a prayer and worship summit.

Five international leaders were in attendance at the prayer gathering. We do not know much about three of them, except what we can determine from the text itself, which is both fairly abundant in information and, in equal measure, frustratingly silent. What we do know about the five men at the prayer meeting is that they were leaders. Luke confirms they were all "prophets and teachers" (v. 1). Both of those designations describe gifted leaders in the early church, just beneath the apostles in rank, authority, or significance. Since the apostles were not part of the Antioch awakening, these men were clearly the leaders of the movement.

The Leaders the Spirit Used (v. 1)

Let's meet these five leaders the Holy Spirit used. First, we know Barnabas. We met him when the church was young and growing rapidly, several years earlier. Barnabas was actually named Joseph; but the apostles were so impressed with his knack for building up other people, they nicknamed him "Son of Encouragement" or, in their language, Barnabas. He was a wealthy Levite from the island of Cyprus who had distinguished himself as a generous leader in the early days of the rapidly growing church (4:36-37). It was his spiritual gift of encouragement that enabled him to see the potential in other people. No wonder God used Barnabas to recruit Saul of Tarsus into full-time ministry in Antioch.

The Holy Spirit's reason for choosing to use a particular individual is not always obvious, but we can see how Barnabas was used by the Spirit. Barnabas blessed and encouraged other people. The Holy Spirit used that gift in his life to encourage a craftsman Barnabas knew from a tent-making guild in Turkey, who, in turn, poured his life into evangelism, discipleship, and missions. The Holy Spirit often mobilizes the church by first mobilizing a handful of passionate leaders.

Clearly Barnabas led the prayer and leaders' summit of Acts 13, but there were some other gifted leaders in the group as well.

For instance, the next prophet/teacher in the prayer group was "Simeon who was called Niger." We don't know everything we might like to know about this man, but his two names give us clues. *Niger* is Latin for "black"; so we might assume, as most do, that Simeon was called *Niger* (pronounced "nī-jər") because he was a dark-skinned man—probably an African disciple. In addition, his original name was Simeon, a Greek-influenced version of the Hebrew name Simon.

Did Luke assume his first readers knew these leaders? Is it possible, as some traditions suggest, that Simeon called Niger is none other than the North African man, Simon of Cyrene, who carried the cross of Jesus? (Luke 23:26). The interesting thing about this supposition revolves around the fact all three Gospels name the man who carried the cross, even though it is only a small portion of Scripture. Why? Wouldn't the story of someone carrying the cross for Jesus be equally as poignant if the man remained anonymous? I see no reason why not. In fact, I have to assume the Gospel writers knew Simon of Cyrene (Cyrene is in North Africa in modern Libya) after he carried the cross, since they all mention his name. Mark goes so far as to mention the name of his two sons, "And they compelled a passerby, Simon of Cyrene, who was coming in from the country, the father of Alexander and Rufus, to carry his cross" (Mark 15:21). Certainly there is no reason to mention the names of the sons unless this family had become known in the early church. It's easy to imagine that Simon's life would never be the same after being conscripted to carry the cross of the Lord. He was thrust into the greatest drama in human history and became an eyewitness to the brutal crucifixion of the Son of God. Can you imagine how that might have affected him? He probably became a follower of Jesus after the resurrection, and his name was known well in the early Christian community.

Why else would the Gospel writers tell us his name? If that interpretation is correct, perhaps the prophet at the prayer meeting—also named Simon and presumably distinguished by his African heritage—could be the same man! If so, Simeon called Niger was probably the only man in that prayer meeting who had seen Jesus of Nazareth in the flesh, face-to-face. Of course, this is speculative, and the information could be interpreted differently.

> The Holy Spirit uses people from every race equally.

In any case, we are starting to get a feel for the international flavor of this group. Barnabas was from an island in the Mediterranean Sea, and Simeon was probably an African. The Holy Spirit uses people from every race equally.

The next man on the list was Lucius of Cyrene. Clearly, Lucius was from the North African nation east of Egypt, known today as Libya. Lucius may have been one of the first evangelists in Antioch. Luke had documented earlier that believers from both Cyprus and Cyrene were among the first wave of evangelical witnesses who settled in Antioch after the deportation (Acts 11:19-21). If that's an accurate piecing together of the clues, the Spirit had found a man of prayer and a soul winner He could use to mobilize the church.

The fourth man listed is an unusual one. Manaen was a "lifelong friend of Herod the tetrarch." The phrase "lifelong friend" is difficult to translate into a comparable English word. It comes from two Greek words, one of which describes a "nursing mother" and the other means "with." Apparently, Manaen was raised in the household of Herod, like a stepbrother or an unrelated member of the family. He was more than a casual friend. What is the significance of this detail provided by Luke?

Herod the tetrarch was a weak, indecisive, immoral, murderous leader who was responsible for the unjust beheading of John the Baptist. He also played a role in Jesus's crucifixion. Even though Herod and Manaen grew up as brothers, their lives took wildly divergent paths. The Holy Spirit mobilizes people into His service regardless of where they come from. Remember, He doesn't call the qualified—He qualifies those He calls!

Saul is mentioned last. He was young and probably the newest member of the group. We know him; he started out terrorizing the church and ended up *building* the church. The Holy Spirit can change anyone, and anyone can be used if they will make themselves available to God.

The Environment That Attracts the Spirit (vv. 2-4)

One of the discernible patterns in Acts is the frequency of prayer meetings that produced dramatic results. The run-up to Pentecost established the design Luke revisited repeatedly in his narrative, where prayer meetings preceded the incredible advances of the early church (Acts 1:14; 4:23-31; 12:5, etc.). The Antioch prayer summit, in keeping with Luke's pattern, preceded the church's first Gentile mission. The strategic shift that occurred after Antioch was as world-changing for the spread of the gospel as Pentecost had been for the birth of the church.

In the Antioch prayer meeting, three spiritual disciplines are highlighted. Verse 2 tells us they were "worshipping the Lord and fasting" (v. 2). The word *worship* means "to serve" and describes the responsibility the priests carried out in the temple to facilitate continuous worship. Practically speaking in this context, "worshipping the Lord" meant the five men were making themselves available to God to be used for His purposes. There are few things we can do that are more effective for inviting the presence of the Spirit than worshipping in an attitude of complete surrender to the purposes of the Lord.

Next, we are told they were "fasting." In the Bible, fasting means we stop eating and, at times, refuse water for a limited period of time. The Greek word for "fasting" comes from the two words that literally mean "no eat." The Old Testament Hebrew word is even more direct: "shut mouth"! The fact they were fasting indicates the prayer meeting was a multiday event. In the Bible there were one-day fasts (Lev. 16:29-31), three-day fasts (Est. 4:16), seven-day fasts (1 Sam. 31:13), twenty-one-day fasts (Dan. 10:3-13), and forty-day fasts (Ex. 24:18; 1 Kings 19:8; Matt. 4:2). We aren't told how long these believers worshipped and fasted, but they were accustomed to fasting; and the fast would hardly seem worth mentioning if it were only a one-day fast, which religious Jews did routinely without mention.

Regardless of the duration of the fast, in Scripture every major fast preceded something new in the kingdom of God. Moses fasted before receiving the Ten Commandments; Elijah fasted before mentoring Elisha; Ezra fasted before journeying across the desert to reestablish proper worship in Jerusalem; and Jesus

65

fasted before beginning His public ministry. The fast in Acts 13 would precede worldwide evangelism!

Finally, they were praying. This environment—worshipping, fasting, and praying—is tailor-made for a visitation from the Holy Spirit! The appearance of the Spirit in verse 2 was profound. During the prayer meeting the Holy Spirit appeared and spoke directly to the group. There are only two other times in Acts (8:29; 10:19) where Luke informs us the "Spirit said." What an incredible moment in history that must have been. The Spirit took the lead in directing the next phase of the work of the church. He instructed the leaders to commission Barnabas and Saul for the "work to which I have called them." That work became known as Paul's first missionary journey, and during that trip Paul started aggressively evangelizing Gentiles. Never before had the church intentionally targeted Gentiles. The Holy Spirit mobilized the church for action!

Extracting promises from narrative literature isn't always the right thing to do, since what God did once with one group of people isn't always what He does with another. But, in Acts, prayer meetings are so consistent as a strategy for ministry, I contend that God intended this method to be the most biblical option available to us in order to see ministry mobilized in our own time. Do you want God to use you? Do you want to see your church mobilized? Do you want the Holy Spirit to lead you?

A friend of mine saw his church grow from about ninety people to over seven thousand in attendance every Sunday. When I asked him how it happened, he told me that he and a few others met to pray every week for God to grow their church. After six months of prayer, one of the men stood up in the prayer meeting and said, "Let's go soul winning!" From that point on, they prayed and shared the gospel regularly, and the church grew.

Admittedly, it's not always that easy, and my friend's church grew over many years. But, when the Spirit wants to get a church on its feet, He looks for a church on its knees. In other words, the Spirit wants to mobilize a praying people. Remember, God isn't concerned with our ability or our inability but with our availability! The Spirit still wants to mobilize your church. Are you available?

---

1 Susan Jacobson, "Firefighters Rescue 66 Riders on Stalled Orlando Eye," *Orlando Sentinel,* July 3, 2015, https://www.orlandosentinel.com /news/breaking-news/os-orlando-eye-stuck-20150703-story.html.

2 I. Howard Marshall, *Acts,* Tyndale New Testament Commentaries (Grand Rapids, MI: Wm. B. Eerdmans, 2000), 200-201.

CHAPTER 5

THE SPIRIT PRAYS FOR THE CHURCH

Romans 8:18-28

Do you ever struggle in prayer? If we are completely honest, we will admit to finding it difficult to pray occasionally. Sometimes we simply don't know how or what to pray.

When I came to Christ during the Jesus movement, revival was in the air. Personal evangelism and the spiritual disciplines of prayer and Bible study were commonly discussed and seemed to be a part of every conversation among the new believers. It was an exciting time. So, when I got serious about my personal growth, I knew from the beginning that prayer was the key to a great relationship with Christ; and that's what I wanted!

I will never forget the first few days of my new walk with God; somebody pushed a tract about prayer into my hand. In it I read about great prayer warriors of the past who prayed hours every day. Their devotion motivated me, so I decided to focus on prayer. I was brand new in my walk with God, but I was determined.

I knelt beside my bed and poured my heart out. I prayed for everything I could think of. I even repeated myself at least once to add more time and weight to the prayer. When I said the final amen, I checked my watch and realized I had prayed for everything I could think of twice; and it only took five minutes! I still had a lot to learn.

Through the years my prayer life has improved, but there are still days and times when prayer seems strangely difficult. Surprisingly, I'm not alone. Even the apostle Paul confessed there were times when he did not know how to pray. If Paul knew how it felt to occasionally struggle in prayer, all of us can expect to have unexpected trouble in prayer from time to time as well.

Here's the good news for all of us: The Holy Spirit prays for the church. The Spirit, therefore, is praying for you, if you are a follower of Christ.

Romans 8 says, "Likewise the Spirit helps us in our weakness. For we do not know what to pray for as we ought, but the Spirit himself intercedes for us with groanings too deep for words. And he who searches hearts knows what is the mind of the Spirit, because the Spirit intercedes for the saints according to the will of God" (vv. 26-27).

The Holy Spirit Chapter (vv. 18-26)

If there's one chapter in Paul's writing we might designate as *the Holy Spirit chapter*, it would, no doubt, be Romans 8. In fact, in all seven chapters of Romans leading up to this chapter, the

Holy Spirit is mentioned two or three times. When we get to chapter 8, however, the Holy Spirit is mentioned nineteen times!

One of those references involves the prayer life of the Holy Spirit. In a passage that may not get enough of our attention, we are assured the Holy Spirit is our *prayer partner.* We might expect the passage to teach the Holy Spirit helps us to pray—and that's true—but it goes deeper than that; the Holy Spirit prays for us! We often hear about praying in the Spirit, but we don't think enough about the Spirit praying in us.

Trouble and Weakness

Even though Romans 8 is bursting with excitement about the Holy Spirit's ministry to us, Paul is transparently honest about inevitable trouble in life. For instance, he referred to this life as "the sufferings of this present time" (v. 18). He mentioned the "futility" of life (v. 20). He even saw all of life as being in "bondage to corruption" (v. 21). Paul's assessments are true: we are weak and face the headwind of opposition in almost every endeavor throughout life.

> The Holy Spirit is our prayer partner.

As a pastor I see the challenges of life constantly. Marriages that look strong on the outside are often hanging together by the slenderest of threads. Children are healthy and happy one moment and in the hospital the next, bringing panic into the lives of parents. Families are stretched to the limit with debt and living paycheck to paycheck, hoping nothing else goes wrong. Funerals are frequent; hearts are broken, and the loss of friends to death reminds us we are separated only by a brief moment before eternity. The list goes on and on. Life is hard.

But there's good news! In the midst of it all, God gives us the privilege of prayer. Through prayer we connect with another world completely. Prayer connects us to God. Unfortunately, our lives are filled with so much trouble that sometimes we don't pray effectively.

I know what it's like to want to pray and find it hard to do. I remember a time when one of our children was in the hospital, and my mind was racing. I wanted to pray, but for a brief time I couldn't control my anxious thoughts long enough to slow down and pray. I've learned this lesson more than once the hard way: at the time when we most need to pray because of life's troubles, we often find it almost impossible to pray due to those same troubles.

So God gives us the Holy Spirit to pray for us. He doesn't just help us pray—He prays for us! It's almost incomprehensible, but it's the promise of God. "Likewise the Spirit helps us in our weakness. For we do not know what to pray for as we ought, but the Spirit himself intercedes for us with groanings too deep for words" (v. 26).

The Holy Spirit helps us in our weakness. "Weakness" in verse 26 comes from a Greek word that means frail, sick, or lacking any strength. Some of us may want to deny any sign of weakness, but over time it gets harder to ignore. My late father was bigger than life to me. He was a big, tall man who was an athletic youth and a rugged outdoorsman in his middle years. He ran a small business and was still happily working long hours into his late seventies. Then, one day, dad had a light stroke from which he never fully recovered. He started walking with a cane. He had trouble getting up from a chair. He said to me, "I'm as weak as pond water." It was a funny, old-fashioned expression; but I knew he wasn't trying to be funny—he was suffering. After being strong and independent all of his life, in his final years his body was uncooperative and weakened. That's the problem with all of us in one way or another. We are weakened spiritually, morally, and physically. Fortunately, God knows how weak we are. So, in mercy, He sends His Holy Spirit in the midst of our weakness; and the Spirit intercedes for us.

Intercession of the Spirit (v. 26)

The Bible says the Spirit intercedes for us, but what is intercession? The idea of intercession is actually similar to our more contemporary word *intervention*. These words are synonyms used to refer to someone voluntarily becoming involved in another person's life.

The word *intercession*, in the original language, describes an action akin to our expression, "He fell in with the wrong crowd." The word literally means to "fall upon," or "light upon a thing." It conjures up the idea of joining with us by "falling in" with us. It's as if God is telling us that while we're stumbling down a path of weakness, failure, and frustration, a powerful friend falls in with us on the journey.

I'm an NBA fan, but my son is a superfan. He keeps me updated about trades and potential trades. A team can be struggling with limited hopes of making the playoffs; but if the right player joins the roster, suddenly everything changes. An entire franchise can be turned around with the addition of a superstar.

73

In a far more profound way, when the Holy Spirit befriends us in our weakness and brings His power to bear upon the challenges we face, our outlook starts to change. In other words, the Spirit's joining us in prayer makes all the difference between success and failure in the Christian life. That's a powerful prayer partner!

How important is prayer if God has assigned the Holy Spirit to engage in it Himself in order to accomplish God's plans for our lives? Prayer is so essential in the accomplishment of God's purposes in the earth that even the Spirit turns to prayer in order to see the Kingdom overcome the troubles that threaten God's children. Prayer is greater than we have ever comprehended. As Jack Taylor once said, "If prayer is anything, prayer is everything."[1] Why wouldn't you ask the Spirit to partner with you in prayer the next time you're struggling?

I'm not a morning person, but I get up early in order to pray. My routine is to rise at 4:00 a.m. every Sunday for prayer and at 4:00 a.m. on one other day each month for a special day of prayer. Most other days I am out of bed at 4:45 a.m. for prayer. I slip into my home office where it's so dark that the moonlight reflecting in my coffee is almost all I can see. In those quiet minutes, I ask the Holy Spirit to help me pray. I thank Him for interceding for me, and I ask Him to make God's will clear to me while I pray. Knowing the Spirit is praying for us changes the way we think about prayer. Scottish pastor and writer Robert Murray M'Cheyne once considered the similar intercessory ministry of Christ and famously said, "If I could hear Christ praying for me in the next room, I would not fear a million of enemies. Yet the distance makes no difference; He is praying for me."[2] The same experience that M'Cheyne described regarding the intercession of Jesus is true of the Spirit as well. We can find assurance of His constant prayer, because we are promised the Holy Spirit has made our business *His* business.

Essentially, when we talk about intercessory prayer, the simple way of understanding it is to picture one person praying for another person. In this case, however, the Holy Spirit is the one praying for us. This is one of His divine assignments! Every time you feel too weak or too scattered or too guilty to pray, rest in this truth: the Holy Spirit is doing what the Father has assigned Him to do. In faith, ask Him to help you pray. He does it, because the Father has assigned Him that responsibility.

The Spirit's intercession does not take the place of your prayers. His prayers assist your prayers. Paul said the Spirit helps us. He didn't say He does it for us. So the primary "weakness" the Holy Spirit intercedes to help overcome is our weakness in prayer. Scripture plainly says, "Likewise the Spirit helps us in our weakness. For we do not know what to pray for as we ought, but the Spirit himself intercedes for us with groanings too deep for words" (v. 26).

The Groanings of the Spirit

What are "groanings too deep for words"? Some may suggest this passage hints at praying in tongues and suppose this entire passage is a description of "praying in the Spirit." A close examination of the text, however, paints a different picture.

Verse 26 is not an example of believers praying in the Spirit; instead, it's an example of the Spirit praying in believers. More importantly, this passage does not describe believers praying with groanings that are inexpressible with words; it describes the Spirit Himself, who is groaning in a way that words can't express. The Spirit's groanings are never heard with our ears. It's how the Spirit prays—in a way unexpressed by words.

"Groaning" may also give us an insider's perspective on the emotions of the Holy Spirit. The Greek root word for groaning implies being constrained or in a straight or narrow place with the idea of restriction and discomfort. In fact, the word for "groan" comes from the Greek word *stenazo*, from which we get our English word *stenographer*, meaning "narrow writing." The word came to mean being grieved due to uncomfortable or *narrowing* circumstances in life. Thus, we get the idea of groaning in sorrow or sighing in grief.

Now, think about what the Holy Spirit *feels* when He observes you in the "sufferings of this present time" (v. 18). He knows when you are in one of those seasons of life when your options narrow due to pain or loss or when your heart is broken; and in those times, when life hurts, what is the Spirit's response? He intercedes for you with a prayer that springs from His grief and sorrow for what you're feeling. He groans and sighs His wordless prayers all the way to the heart of God.

In addition to the deep compassion the Holy Spirit feels for God's people, He never goes off duty. In fact, the language itself speaks to the persistence of the Spirit's intercession. There are two action words in verse 26 that are relative to the Spirit's ministry of prayer, which should fill us with hope. Paul tells us the Spirit both "helps us" and "intercedes for us." Both of these words are present-tense verbs. By describing these ministries to the body of Christ in the present tense, Paul makes it clear they are perpetual, ongoing, and consistent. The Spirit doesn't take breaks. He doesn't stop helping, and He doesn't stop interceding.

When I was a college student, a young athlete on our campus was saved and started growing in Christ immediately. He and I became close friends, and we prayed together frequently. Eventually he went to the international mission field in Asia, where he has remained for many years. After he had been there for a decade, he called me to catch up. During the conversation he told me he had prayed for me every day since we had been friends in school. I was stunned. To think of a man, whom I hadn't seen in more than a decade, faithfully praying for me every day through all those years was a humbling experience. I almost didn't know what to say in response. It was a meaningful moment.

Have you had someone praying for you like that? Perhaps a parent has been praying for you every day for years. Maybe your spouse continually prays for you. It's a powerfully rewarding feeling to know someone prays for you daily.

Paul's use of present-tense verbs relative to the Spirit's ministry of prayer is significant. The Spirit never stops praying for the church. During every good day, and through every challenge, the Holy Spirit has been praying for the people who follow Jesus. Be encouraged: your heavenly prayer partner is on the job!

When we consider the incredible significance of the Spirit praying for us, we may be tempted to ask why the Spirit utters His intercession in "groanings" that defy vocabulary and language. Perhaps the short answer is: He isn't talking to us. Apparently, we do not need to comprehend the Spirit's prayers or the language He chooses in order to communicate with the Father. It is enough to know the Father and Spirit speak the same language. They are in constant dialogue about us. The Spirit offers His groans on our behalf, and our Father hears and understands.

The Spirit and the Will of God (v. 27)

Why do we pray? There are several reasons: We want to fellowship with God, and prayer is one of the best ways to do that. When we confess our sins, it is through prayer. Thanking God requires prayer. There are many reasons why we pray, but one of the most common reasons for prayer involves our desire to know the will of God.

Have you ever wanted to know God's will? Did you pray about it? As I was writing these words, I received a text message from a friend asking for prayer about a significant family issue that appears to have no easy answers. The friend needed to know the will of God in order to take action, so he requested prayer. Our church receives similar prayer requests every day. People want to know God's will. The problem—the inherent weakness we all have concerning God's will—is clear: we cannot know the future, and so much of God's plan is around the corner or off in the more distant future.

An unclear future can paralyze us with uncertainty as we pray. Fortunately, the Holy Spirit does not suffer from limitations related to the future. In fact, His insights are so much greater than ours as to be incomparable. He prays in sync with God the Father, who constantly dialogues with the mind of the Spirit.

The Holy Spirit intercedes for us according to the will of God. That means, among other things, the Spirit never wastes time praying for the wrong outcomes. Have you ever prayed for something that you later came to believe was not God's will? My car alerts me with short beeps when I drive too close to the edge of the road or when a car is passing me. The first time my wife rode in the car with me, she asked innocently, "What is all that noise?" While the beeping sounds can be a little irritating, they exist for the purpose of reminding me to stay in my lane. Wouldn't it be nice if we had some kind of force in life that helped us stay focused on the right way to move and act? We do. The Holy Spirit is constantly praying for us to keep our lives aligned with the will of God!

> The Holy Spirit prays for us to keep our lives aligned with God's will.

Have you ever looked back on your life and thought how a seemingly small decision at the time turned out to be a determining factor in what your life is becoming now? When Cliff Barrows and his wife got married in the summer of 1945 in California, the young Christian couple decided to honeymoon in the mountains of Asheville, North Carolina. While they were there, they learned of a Youth for Christ event nearby; so they attended, only to be drafted into service. The piano player and song leader who was scheduled to lead worship was unexpectedly summoned back to Chicago. The speaker that night was the twenty-six-year-old evangelist Billy Graham. Graham was scrambling for a backup plan and was told Barrows could lead music and his new bride could play the piano. So, with no other options and time running out, Billy Graham asked a man he didn't know—Cliff Barrows—to lead worship. That series of "coincidences" led to one of the most famous partnerships that would span seven decades.[3]

What if the young couple hadn't decided to attend the service? What if the regular song director hadn't been suddenly called away? The "what ifs" are endless, but God's leadership is clear. It's obviously easier to look back at a story like Billy Graham accidentally meeting Cliff Barrows and see God's guiding hand, but the same Spirit who knows the will of God in famous people's lives knows the will of God for our lives too. So, no matter what we may be praying about at any given time, the Holy Spirit acts as a kind of *guardrail* to protect us and keep us aligned with God's actual intention and direction for our lives because He prays according to the will of God.

The Purposes of God (v. 28)

Perhaps no verse in Romans is more well-known or more frequently quoted than Romans 8:28. It is a verse filled with reassurances that no matter what may happen, God still has a good plan for His people. What may be less known is its context. The first word of Romans 8:28 is "and." Big truths sometimes hang on little words. The word *and* is a connecting word that shows the continuation of a thought. "And we know that for those who love God all things work together for good, for those who are called according to his purpose" (v. 28).

Paul had just explained the almost unexplainable—the Holy Spirit is on duty praying for the church in accordance with God's will (vv. 26-27). Now, in verse 28, he explains how the will of God is accomplished. His will is explicitly connected to the

Spirit's intercession. We are assured that after all of His intercession on our behalf, there is an outcome that is guaranteed. God hears all of the Spirit's prayers for us and works everything *for our good.*

Romans 8:28 has tremendous theological implications and serves as an introduction to the doctrine of divine predestination in verse 29 and following. Christians often disagree on the meaning of the word *predestination.* Regardless of how one interprets the biblical teaching on predestination, however, it is clear from this passage that at least part of the doctrine teaches that God planned from the beginning to vindicate His people at some point in the future, when He finally works all things for their good. What may get lost in the debate about predestination and foreknowledge, themes that are introduced by verses 28 through 30, is the fact that Romans 8:28 is first and foremost an answer to prayer. The Spirit's prayers are answered this way: God takes every situation and circumstance in our lives and bends them in the direction of what is ultimately for our good. Not every situation is good; but in response to the Spirit's intercession, God *uses* everything for our good! He has predestined it to be so. The Spirit's intercession is part of God's larger plan.

What are you going through today? How big are the biggest things beating down on you? How frightened are you of the scariest enemies you face? What shadow of "this present darkness" is the most haunting from your perspective? Whatever it may be, the Holy Spirit has it targeted on His prayer list, and God has predestined His answer: He is going to cause it all to work for your good.

Through the years I have accumulated a lot of books on the subject of prayer. One of my favorites is a collection of stories about answered prayer. The testimonies of answered prayer encourage us to press on in prayer. Occasionally we all need to be reminded that our prayers are being heard, even if the answers are slow (by our impatient standards) in coming.

Fortunately, we have an assurance: even if our personal prayers are weak or timid, or even if we rarely see the answers we're hoping for, the Holy Spirit is always praying for us. As a result, God is going to answer every prayer of the Spirit in a way that turns out best for us!

The incredible promise of the Spirit's intercession is not given to a special class of Christians who maintain a powerful prayer life. Instead, it's a promise to every believer in the body of Christ. Even if your prayer life is far less committed than you know it should be, the Holy Spirit has never stopped interceding on your behalf. Let the truth of God's promise motivate you to pray more and pray with more faith, because your invisible prayer partner is still on the job!

---

1 Jack Taylor, *Prayer: Life's Limitless Reach* (Nashville: Broadman Press, 1977), introduction, paragraph seven.

2 Andrew Bonar, *The Biography of Robert Murray M'Cheyne* (n.p.: Pantianos Classics, 2018), 126-127.

3 William Martin, *A Prophet With Honor: The Billy Graham Story* (New York: William Morrow & Company, 1991), 94.

CHAPTER 6

THE SPIRIT TEACHES THE CHURCH

1 Corinthians 2:1-16

President Barack Obama had come to the podium to speak. The stadium in Johannesburg, South Africa was packed with ninety-five thousand people who had gathered for the memorial service for Nelson Mandela. Standing beside the American president was the sign language interpreter who had been hired for the occasion. The world was watching the service on television and was mostly unaware, but people from the deaf community knew something was dramatically wrong and embarrassingly inappropriate. There, in front of millions of people, the interpreter was making wild hand gestures that corresponded to no sign language.

He looked harmless enough—short, rotund, baby-faced, and calm. He was wearing a conservative blue suit, which was appropriate attire for the somber occasion of the funeral for one of the world's most revered leaders. But standing there that day, unknown to anyone else, the interpreter was suffering from hallucinations. The internal mental chaos he was experiencing took his performance off the rails. His bizarre signs were the equivalent of gibberish, created in a world of his own. They made no sense.

The thirty-four-year-old imposter, Thamsanqa Jantjie, later admitted he had recently been released from a psychiatric hospital for violent tendencies due to schizophrenia and had witnessed angels descending on the stadium that day. The entire incident was an embarrassment for the South African government, who had hired Jantjie for an unusually low fee, a bargain really, from an unknown company that disappeared without a trace after the funeral.[1]

For at least six thousand years since the Mesopotamians developed a kind of alphabet, creating symbols that corresponded to their spoken language, people have been reading.[2] If you know the alphabet and the language the symbols represent, you can understand the symbols and what they intend to communicate. You're doing it now. You look at repetitive, black blotches of ink against white paper or little digital images on a glass screen and somehow what you see corresponds in your brain to something else you have seen or heard. As a result, communication takes place because the symbols make sense.

Understanding the words around us is important, since they guide our daily lives. For instance, if you should go to a nice restaurant in Tokyo, and your waiter recommends a popular item called *basashi* from the menu because it's popular and highly recommended, you might order it, even though you don't know what it is. After all, you want to try new things, right? But you might be surprised when your meal arrives. In Japan, *basashi*—a real delicacy—means raw horse meat. A lot of people in Tokyo like it. You probably won't.

Here's the problem: If you don't recognize the symbols or letters or you don't know how to interpret the words you read or hear, you obviously won't understand what the sign language interpreter is signing or what the menu is describing. Communication hasn't really occurred if the one listening or reading doesn't understand the message as it's spoken or read. Even worse, if the communicator is signing or writing gibberish, we may form a conclusion; but it likely won't be the one the writer or communicator had hoped for!

The Bible has been translated into hundreds of languages. Looking at my own bookshelves right now, for instance, I can see at least ten different English translations. The Bible app on my phone has even more. There are still languages that need a Bible translation, obviously; but if you're reading this you probably have access to a Bible in a language you understand.

Surprisingly, as important as Bible translation is as a tool for missions and evangelism and as the backbone for Christian discipleship, comprehending the meaning of words in your own language is only one component of understanding the Bible. Paul taught the need for the Spirit's ministry at work in the reader if we are really going to grasp the meaning of Scripture. In fact, he insisted no one can understand the Word of God apart from the Holy Spirit's help.

Let me put it bluntly: If the Spirit doesn't illuminate the mind of the person reading the Bible, the message of God's

Word is as meaningless to the reader as Thamsanqa Jantjie's hallucination-inspired, erratic hand gestures at Mandela's funeral. The Bible is truth without any mixture of error, but the person reading the Bible without the Holy Spirit's help is incapable spiritually of grasping its life-giving message. How do I know? Because the Bible tells me so.

The Need We Never Outgrow (2:1-3)

The professor stood in front of his packed class on the first day of the semester, opened his Greek New Testament, and translated multiple verses perfectly into English from the third chapter of John, including the famous and meaningful John 3:16. Then he said, "That's good theology if you believe it, but I don't." At that point in his well-rehearsed and dramatic introduction, the professor dropped his Greek New Testament into the garbage can.

As a seminary student, one picks up a lot of stories like that one, allegedly true, which I heard years ago while I was in seminary about a well-known professor at another university. If it is true, and I have no reason to doubt that it actually happened, the story speaks in bright colors about a need overlooked so easily, even by the faithful. The Bible is not understood merely because it is translated for us into the language we speak, even *if,* we can translate it ourselves from the original languages. The words may be read artfully and comprehended linguistically, but the message is lost if the Holy Spirit doesn't help us understand it. We need the Spirit to teach us.

Paul wrote to the Corinthians with a level of frustration sometimes felt by parents when their children stubbornly refuse to live up to their potential and choose, instead, to coast along beneath their talents. The Corinthians were like those children. They were a gifted and greatly loved congregation; but pride, infighting, and sectarianism threatened to divide their church and ruin their witness in the city. In order to both confront and correct the church he had planted, Paul began by reminding them how they started in the first place.

Paul had arrived in Corinth with apprehension about how to engage the culture and effectively share the gospel (v. 1). He knew their sophisticated training in Greek philosophy would make them a naturally skeptical audience. So he did something radical; he stuck to one central theme—a theme sure to raise elite eyebrows in an erudite and cosmopolitan city such as Corinth. Paul preached the message of the crucifixion of Jesus. He deliberately avoided sophistry and philosophical debates and, instead, focused on a plain message delivered in the power of the Holy Spirit (vv. 2-4).

> No one can understand the Word of God apart from the Holy Spirit's help.

After reminding the Corinthians about their shared past and chiding them about their divisive cliques (1:11-13), Paul moved on to the subject of the Spirit's role in interpreting the message of the gospel and, by extension, the entire message of the Bible. Even if they were able to overcome their petty factionalism, if they didn't understand the Word of God and, worse yet, understand *how* to understand the Word of God, they would continually be led down dead ends of false doctrine and ineffective witness. Only by recognizing the role of the Holy Spirit in reading and interpreting the Word could they hope to grow into the mature believers they were called to become.

We are no different today. We haven't learned enough or matured enough or outgrown our need for the Holy Spirit's illumination of the Word. We will never outgrow our need for the Spirit's help in understanding the Word. If we hope to understand the Word correctly, the Holy Spirit must teach us.

God Speaks (vv. 9-16)

God's revelation begins and ends beyond even the best human ideas. Yet, because He wants us to know and experience His plans, He has explained what eyes haven't seen before, ears haven't heard before, and no one has imagined before (vv. 9-10). Paul said the unimaginable blessings of God have been "revealed to us through the Spirit" (v. 10).

The word "revealed" in verse 10 is the Greek word *apokalupto*, from which we get our English word *apocalypse*. While in common vernacular we tend to think of an apocalypse as some dreaded end-time scenario, that's not its real meaning at all. Instead, *apokalupto* means "that which is uncovered" or "taken out of hiding."

Everything God has for His church is brought to light from His otherwise mysterious, unknown thoughts and uncovered in plain sight. The agency by which His revelation occurs has never been human ingenuity or wisdom. No one simply thinks about God's plan long enough and then *figures it out* on their own. We can only understand the wisdom of God by the power of the Holy Spirit (v. 10). We don't comprehend spiritual truth by human intellect, collective conscience, group think, or by being the smartest guy in the room. God makes clear the only way to grasp the unexplored realities of the other world is by the Holy Spirit.

The reason for this is explained by way of a powerful analogy. Paul reminds us, for example, that only a person is intimate with his own thoughts until he is willing to reveal them (v. 11). We may guess what others are thinking by their actions, through knowledge of their past history, or because we can guess future behavior based on human nature; but the truth is we can never really know the inner thoughts of other people. Those secrets can only be revealed to us by the other person.

The same is true of God. His thoughts are, as the prophet reminds us, "not our thoughts" (Isa. 55:8). In other words, God's wisdom and insights are so far above our most elevated concepts, we would be more likely to jump from our beds each morning and touch the rings of Saturn than we would be able to comprehend the deep inner and inscrutable thoughts of God (1 Cor. 2:10-11).

How, therefore, can we ever understand God or know His will or grow in the knowledge of His Word? The answer is supplied to us: God's Spirit searches the thoughts of God and reveals to us the mind of God (v. 11).

Every day, like millions of other people, I enter words into a search engine to locate some kind of information from the Internet. In seconds I am presented with web pages, articles, and options so fast it's unbelievable. For instance, as I was writing this (to illustrate my point) I typed the word *Baptist* into my search engine and in 0.69 seconds I received 270,000,000 results. That's a lot of Baptists!

In a similar way, when you or I are contemplating an action or a thought, our minds are processing images, stimuli, memories, and other data faster than we can articulate the process. We do, after all, think at the speed of thought. Most of us would acknowledge that in some weird and unexplainable way we are able not only to think but to simultaneously think about the fact we are thinking! We have our own built-in "search engines," allowing us to think about what we're thinking. Human beings, created in the image of God, are innately intelligent, curious, analytical, and deeply aware of our own thoughts. No wonder René Descartes built his philosophy on the bedrock of *Cogito ergo sum*—"I think therefore I am."[3]

Delving too deeply into the details of philosophy, psychiatry, or neuroscience is beyond the scope of this writer and this chapter; but it is commonly accepted that we understand the brain better than we understand the mind.[4] To put this conversation into a biblical framework, however, we notice Paul called the function of the searching and analytical capacity of the mind the "spirit" within us. For Paul, the "spirit" of a human being may involve more than the mind; but it, at least, seems to include the function of consciousness and personal awareness. In other words, in addition to the role of the Holy Spirit, our own human spirit interacts within us at a deeply intrinsic, personal level, searching our own thoughts. In this way, we are constantly, consciously, and subconsciously evaluating our own thoughts. In the same way, the Holy Spirit searches the mind of God.

In a way not unlike the way our human spirits search, analyze, and categorize our private thoughts, the Holy Spirit searches the mind of God. Furthermore, He accurately "comprehends" the thoughts of God, and no one but the Spirit of God is capable of this feat (v. 11). In other words, there is a depth of knowledge and insight that is totally unavailable to us apart from the Holy Spirit's illumination of God's Word.

Even if you had a Doctor of Philosophy degree in Greek and Hebrew, and even though you could easily read the Bible, apart from the Spirit no one can understand the real message of God! If you think that seems somehow unfair or capricious on God's part, let me clarify: The goodness of God is revealed in the fact that we are given the ability, by the Spirit, to comprehend the deep truths of God in the first place. God does not owe us anything. He chooses to reveal Himself and His thoughts. If He did not reveal Himself, we could not comprehend Him any more than a newborn baby can write a doctoral dissertation on hermeneutics.

The challenge, therefore, is simple enough to grasp: How can the infinite God—the divine Logos, the Mind behind everything—talk to small, finite minds such as mine? He speaks to us by His Word, explained by His Spirit. There is simply no other way.

Our Response

Since God wants to reveal Himself and communicate with us, we should be willing to listen and be as receptive as possible. We should press in to know Him and hear Him. How? For the purposes of this discussion about the Spirit and the Word, I suggest two practical steps. First, since the Spirit illuminates the Word of God, we should become as familiar as possible with the Bible. We must read God's Word to know Him. Remember: where Scripture speaks, God speaks.

Reading books about the Bible (such as the one you're reading now) is an extremely beneficial exercise, but reading the Bible itself is far more important. So here's a fundamental question: Do you have a plan for reading Scripture?

To mature in the Christian life, every believer should read from the Bible every day. There's no practical advantage to us if we affirm that the Spirit illuminates the Word but don't read it. A reading plan helps: having the right tools available, the right time scheduled, and the right texts chosen.

Tools

Choose your Bible. Translations differ, and you should find one you enjoy reading. As a pastor, when asked, I recommend a modern language version. Currently I study and preach from the English Standard Version. It is readable, and it is designed to be a bit more literal than the New International Version. Another translation I like is the Christian Standard Bible published in 2017. It reads easily; and, like the ESV, it utilizes a more literal approach to translation.

Another tool almost any believer can acquire is a Bible dictionary. Many of the questions the reader might have about a text can be answered quickly with a Bible dictionary. Get one that is illustrated to add to the learning experience. I use the latest edition of the *Holman Illustrated Bible Dictionary.*

Many other Bible study tools could be mentioned here; but, at the very least, you should have a system of taking and keeping notes as you read. Everything from writing in your Bible, highlighting or underlining passages, to keeping a journal of questions and observations about what you're reading and studying can be helpful. God will speak to you as you read the Word, so recording your thoughts can be a powerful asset.

Time

God deserves your time. Everything of importance in our life is scheduled. You know when a new semester starts, when a doctor's appointment is planned, or what time you're supposed to be at work. We shouldn't leave Bible study to chance or develop the attitude that says, "I will read it if I get the time." Schedule your Bible study every day at a set time, and keep your appointment with God. By making this simple adjustment, setting a specific time for Bible reading, you will develop greater consistency.

Text

What text are you going to read? Eventually you will want to complete the entire Bible, and excellent resources are available to guide you through the entire Bible in a year. Your Bible may even include a reading plan within its pages. You can read the New Testament in a shorter time and, perhaps, that would be an excellent place to start. At the very least, you should choose a specific Bible reading plan, such as reading and studying the book of John, Romans, Psalms, or Genesis. Develop good reading and study practices until Bible study becomes a more reliable habit. For instance, you may decide to read one chapter of the New Testament every day, at a minimum. I have a minimum number of

God speaks to us by His Word, explained by His Spirit.

chapters of Scripture I read every day; and I have never missed a day since 1980. Having the discipline of a plan is simple but super important for continued success. Decide what you'll read, how much you'll read, and when you'll read. As a result, you *will* read!

The Spirit

The second practical step in your growth strategy relates to the Holy Spirit. Since God's Spirit is our teacher, we should be as familiar with the Holy Spirit as possible. At the very least, pray before reading the Scripture, asking the Spirit to fill you and speak to you as you read.

If you remain open to a relationship with the Holy Spirit, and if you read the Bible regularly, there will be breakthrough moments when you will know the Spirit is teaching you and opening up the Word to you in a fresh way. Years ago, when I was beginning my walk with God, I was confronted with some doctrinal teaching I could not understand. Christian friends challenged my thinking, and I knew the answer was in the Bible. So every day for weeks I read one chapter of Scripture where the doctrine was discussed. At first, as a new believer, I simply did not understand the teaching; but I kept reading this passage daily, asking the Lord to help me "get" it. One night, while reading that same passage, it struck me like a lightning bolt. I *suddenly* saw it. What didn't make sense to me before immediately opened to me. How did I miss it?

What happened? For one thing, as a new believer I still had a lot to learn. I had plenty of this world's ideology still floating through my head, but I wanted God to change me and speak to me. So, by saturating my mind and my spirit with God's Word, the Holy Spirit gave me a spiritual breakthrough!

As we walk in the Spirit and consistently read the Word, those breakthroughs continue to occur. God's Spirit uses the Word of God to mold our thinking into conformity with God's will for us. Why would we ever want to live without that process working in our lives?

The Spirit Who Creates (vv. 12-13)

If there's one secret about the pastorate every pastor knows, but few others fully appreciate, it is the amount of study and writing every pastor does each week. For instance, if your pastor preaches even twice a week, over a ministry's lifetime he will have written more than the most recent edition of the entire *Encyclopedia Britannica*! Few authors crank out as much new material as your pastor.

If you add to that the blogs, magazine articles, and books we write, it starts to add up. There are times when I feel all I do is generate and create new content. Of course, that's not all I do; but after almost thirty years as a senior pastor, I have learned the rigors of constant content creation. Have you ever thought about the Holy Spirit as an author? His work is more well-known than any *New York Times* best-selling author. The Holy Spirit wrote the world's best seller—the Bible. Can anyone explain what a book is about better than the author can?

When writing to the Corinthians, Paul made some incredible claims about the Spirit and the Word of God. "Now we have received not the spirit of the world, but the Spirit who is from God, that we might understand the things freely given us by God.

And we impart this in words not taught by human wisdom but taught by the Spirit, interpreting spiritual truths to those who are spiritual" (vv. 12-13).

Notice the family of ideas expressed in Paul's words in verses 12 and 13. He develops a related concept through the words "understand," "taught," "wisdom," "interpreting," and "truths." Clearly, the Holy Spirit has a major role in our development as believers. Through the Holy Spirit's ministry we can grasp truth instead of falsehood, and He gives us wisdom through teaching and a right interpretation of God's Word. We are not born again with every answer already preprogrammed into our thoughts. We have to learn, and the Holy Spirit is our teacher and interpreter of God's truth.

So what do we need to do to have this level of access to the Spirit? Actually, Paul uses the word "received" to describe our relationship to the Spirit (v. 12). When you became saved you received the indwelling Holy Spirit. You already have the Holy Spirit living inside your life if you are a born-again follower of Jesus.

We have "received" the Holy Spirit. It is important not to undervalue our role in interacting with the Spirit and developing our relationship with the Spirit, in spite of the fact He already indwells every believer (Rom. 8:9). Why do I say this? For one thing, the Spirit is a person with personal traits. For instance, we can "grieve" the Holy Spirit by our negligent words, attitudes, and actions (Eph. 4:29-31). In addition, we can "quench" the Spirit (1 Thess. 5:19). Quenching something is like extinguishing a flame. When the Holy Spirit is active and moving freely in our lives, the Word of God seems alive and dynamic. But when we allow sin and worldly attitudes to drive our lives, the Holy Spirit's activity in us is resisted, grieved, and even quenched! I wonder whether a lot of believers are shallow in their faith and understanding of God's plan simply because their lifestyle resists the instruction and gentle leadership of the Holy Spirit. If you want the Spirit to open up the deep things of God, you can't remain in a shallow relationship with the Holy Spirit! The more you submit to the Spirit's role in your life, the more you're going to receive truth from God's Word. It is inevitable.

The Spirit wrote the Book, and He will always be the best teacher of the Book! The Spirit saved you (John 3:6-7), and the Spirit wrote the Bible; and when He puts the child of God He birthed together with the Word of God He authored, there is bound to be spontaneous combustion. You will receive God's truth. You were made for it.

The Spirit of the Word (vv. 14-16)

Lost people cannot grasp the truth of God. Paul was as direct as possible regarding this fact. He wrote, "The natural person does not accept the things of the Spirit of God, for they are folly to him, and he is not able to understand them because they are spiritually discerned" (v. 14). Paul wanted the Corinthians, and all of us, to accept the fact the world around us cannot understand the Word of God because they are living in their "natural," which is to say, their unregenerate, state of being. Therefore, we should never be surprised when lost people think lost, spend lost, react lost, and talk lost. They're lost. Only when we evangelize the lost and they receive Christ do they receive the Spirit and the capacity to understand the Word of God.

One day I was with a particular a group of people. As we were preparing to go our separate ways, I asked one of the guys to stay for a while longer. When he asked me why, I half-jokingly responded, "So we can read the Bible." He was not a Christian and shot back, "Man, the last thing I'm going to do tonight is read the Bible!" We laughed; but, with that sliver of an opening, I started an evangelistic conversation, which couldn't have gone better. After several questions and answers, and a good conversation about God's offer of salvation by faith alone, he confessed his sin and invited Christ into his life.

> The Holy Spirit leads the entire congregation of God's people to the Word of God.

I immediately challenged him to grow in the Lord by reading the Bible, praying, attending church, and sharing his faith. He seemed anxious to get started; so I handed him my Bible, opened it to the Gospel of John, and encouraged him to read the first chapter. He did.

As I walked away, I couldn't help but smile. Less than an hour earlier he had declared, "The last thing I'm going to do tonight is read the Bible"; and guess what? He was right. The last thing he did that night was read the Bible!

When people are saved, the Spirit begins immediately giving them a hunger and an appetite for truth; and God's Word supplies the truth our souls crave. The Holy Spirit leads the entire congregation of God's people to the Word of God. The Spirit interprets the Word to our hearts. The Spirit uses the Word to teach the church what God wants us everyone to know.

1 Nicholas Kulish, John Eligon, and Alan Cowell, "Interpreter at Mandela Service Says He Is Schizophrenic and Saw Angels Descend," *New York Times*, December 12, 2013, https://www.nytimes.com/2013/12/13/world/africa/mandela-memorial-interpreter.html.

2 Maria Popova, "A History of Reading," Brainpickings, October 26, 2012, https://www.brainpickings.org/2012/10/26/a-history-of-reading/.

3 "Descartes: 'I Think Therefore I Am'," New Learning: Transformational Design for Pedagogy and Assessment, accessed December 6, 2018, http://newlearningonline.com/new-learning/chapter-7/descartes-i-think-therefore-i-am.

4 Sally Satel, "Distinguishing Brain From Mind," Health, *The Atlantic*, May 30, 2013, https://www.theatlantic.com/health/archive/2013/05/distinguishing-brain-from-mind/276380/.

CHAPTER

7

THE SPIRIT EQUIPS
THE CHURCH

1 Corinthians 12

When I heard that Billy Graham was planning to preach at First Baptist Church in Dallas, I decided to attend. It was in the early 1980s. I was a seminary student in nearby Fort Worth; so the chance to see the evangelist in a church, instead of a stadium, seemed like too good an opportunity to pass up.

Tina and I left Fort Worth extremely early that Sunday morning so we could get good seats. Even though we arrived an hour early for church, the pews were full; so we stood along the wall to the right of the platform on the lower floor. It was a great view and fairly close to the pulpit in the historic, old sanctuary.

In those days I had a nice Nikon camera with a zoom lens, so I took it along to get close-up pictures of my favorite preacher. The angles I captured were perfect. Every time Billy Graham made one of his famous gestures—a long finger pointed at the congregation, the Bible held high, his head bowed in prayer while rested on his closed hand with arms folded—I snapped a picture.

The camera made a little metallic, clicking noise as I snapped each photo and manually advanced the film for the next shot. My wife was uncomfortable, because she thought I was too noisy and too obvious while taking pictures in church. No one else was taking pictures. I was probably distracting others. She was giving me a look that silently communicated I had taken enough pictures. I was a little intimidated myself, but when would I get an opportunity to be this close to Billy Graham again? So I ignored the embarrassment of noisily taking picture after picture.

I would love to show you those special photographs, but I can't. I had no film in my camera that day. In my excitement about taking personal, close-up pictures of Billy Graham, I had skipped an important step. I'm still feeling a little sheepish about that entire episode!

Anytime we start a project, if we want to reach our goal, it is essential to have the right tools. Sure, I've used dimes for screwdrivers and books stacked on chairs instead of a ladder a few times, but nothing works better than the equipment designed for the job. Whether it's Kodachrome in your Nikon or a flathead screwdriver instead of a butter knife, the right equipment often spells the difference between merely doing it and actually doing it right.

In the Christian life, the church has a choice to make. We can attempt to serve the Lord with our natural talents and human strategies or we can operate in the supernatural realm, as the early church did in the New Testament. The difference all comes down to the right equipment. The Holy Spirit is ready to equip every believer, young or old, with the powerful, spiritual gifts that are available to everyone in the body of Christ. I've actually tried it both ways over the course of my ministry. The spiritual way is better!

Yes, You Are Gifted (vv. 4-7)

Do you remember the struggles addressed in the book of 1 Corinthians? Paul was obviously frustrated with the church for their lack of unity and undisciplined behavior (3:1-3). They were all new Christians, and they hadn't matured much. Later in the book, Paul challenged their toleration of blatant sexual immorality (5:1-13). Still later, he called them out for selfishness, gluttony, and drunkenness at the Lord's Supper service (11:17-22).

The church at Corinth had issues. In fact, it was a mess. Can you imagine what the unchurched community would have said about the Christians at the Corinthian church if they would have had Twitter? Today, because the Corinthians' sins and blunders were so publicly disgraceful, we would read about them in the headlines of the tabloid newspapers sold at the checkout counters in the grocery stores. Through the ages no church has been held up as a bad example more often than the immature and worldly believers at Corinth.

So why do we need to review the Corinthians' spiritual dirty laundry? What's the point? That's a fair question, and here's why: they were a highly gifted church, and their spiritual immaturity did not prohibit them from discovering, developing, and deploying their incredible spiritual gifts. Paul had numerous correctives to share with the spiritually infantile congregation, but he never suggested they didn't have spiritual gifts or they shouldn't have pursued them (12:27-31; 14:1-12).

Here's the point for us: If that immature and often sinful congregation had spiritual gifts, so do you—if you're a follower of Jesus. The gifts are part of the package God gives His entire church by the power of the Holy Spirit in order to equip us for ministry. No believer is exempt.

I was preaching a sermon series a few years ago on the subject of spiritual gifts when an older member of the congregation approached me and said, "Pastor, I don't think I have any spiritual gifts." In my exuberance, I half-jokingly exclaimed, "Then you must not be saved!" He didn't think it was funny. I have to add that flippant comment to the long list of things I shouldn't have said along the way. I wasn't questioning the man's heart for God in that interaction, but the statement I made is actually correct. Since *every* believer has spiritual gifts, the people who do not have spiritual gifts are unbelievers—those who are not followers of Jesus. So, if you're saved, the Holy Spirit has given you spiritual gifts.

Even though every believer has a spiritual gift, and often more than one, believers are sometimes confused about the gifts. Can a person actually have spiritual gifts and not know it? Yes, in a sense. For instance, one of the best Bible teachers I have ever known told me a few years ago she didn't know what her spiritual gifts were. She, obviously, had teaching gifts, but she didn't know it. In a church where the gifts are not taught or encouraged, believers can actually operate in their gifts with no awareness of what they are or how they are discerned, even when they are familiar with other biblical doctrines. I believe many gifted believers operate in the gifts simply because they have them by grace, even though they have not been taught much about them. My own spiritual gifts were in operation long before I realized what was happening. In fact, I thought every believer had my instincts for the kinds of ministry I gravitated toward. My gifts were leading me, even before I knew they were spiritual gifts.

In spite of what many people don't know, this much is certain: Every believer is gifted by the Holy Spirit to operate in their gifting in order to build up the body of Christ and share Him with the world (v. 7). The Holy Spirit has built the church to operate through our spiritual gifts.

The Spirit Manifests the Gifts (vv. 7-11)

The darkness was so complete it was unimaginable. Tina and I were on a tour of Mammoth Cave. When we had gone to the deepest part of the underground cavern, the tour guide instructed us to cover our watches so no light could be seen from the luminous dials. All the lights in the cave were then turned off. I had never experienced such complete darkness before, or since. Then, after a few moments, the tour guide asked if we were ready for the lights to come back on; the group all said yes. At that point she did something unexpected. She lit a single, wooden match. In the absence of all other light, the little match illuminated the entire area where our group of twenty or more people stood. Light changes everything.

Paul said our gifts are a "manifestation of the Spirit" (v. 7). The word "manifestation" translates a Greek word that everyone will recognize. Its basic root word is *phos*, from which we get the English words "photograph," "photosynthesis," "phosphorous," and numerous other words that have something to do with light. The word *manifest* means "to bring a thing into the light."

Imagine this: The Holy Spirit is "brought to light" when the church is operating in its gifts! When you use your spiritual gift, you are inviting the manifestation of the Holy Spirit into whatever your circumstance at the time. Put another way, your spiritual gifts ignite the light of the Spirit into the darkness of the world.

Every believer is gifted by the Holy Spirit.

Spiritual gifts are a witness to the dark world. When you recognize your gifts and start operating in them, the Spirit is manifested through the ministries you perform. This is a critical distinction: Your spiritual gifts are not given to cast a light on you. Spiritual gifts shine the light on the Holy Spirit and His activities. Just think about the outcome if thousands of Christians were manifesting the Holy Spirit every day in their cities through the consistent ministry of all of their spiritual gifts.

Paul gives us a second reason why every believer in the body of Christ needs to use their spiritual gifts: Each of us is given a spiritual gift "for the common good" (v. 7). A literal translation of the phrase "common good" gives us the idea of people bearing with one another or, perhaps, carrying each other. In other words, the concept of "the common good" translates the idea of mutual support on behalf of another. When you use your spiritual gifts, therefore, it is for the support and uplifting of others, not for yourself. A friend of mine often says he wishes we translated spiritual gifts as spiritual tools since gifts may imply something for our amusement, when, in fact, they are given to help us do our work. Our gifts are used for the improvement of our community and our culture.

Can you imagine a time in your life when the church has needed the Spirit-empowered ministry of mutual support more than we do now? All of us should pray for an outpouring of the Spirit throughout the body of Christ so that as a people we can rise to the occasion of ministry for "the common good."

The Spirit Distributes Different Gifts (vv. 8-10)

Like every other doctrine in the New Testament, no one passage explains everything about the spiritual gifts. Besides the insights provided to the Corinthians, the other relevant passages related to spiritual gifts are found in Romans 12:6-8, Ephesians 4:11, and 1 Peter 4:11. When we review these lists, while recognizing and accounting for some overlap and repetition among them, we can identify just over twenty individual, unique gifts. The focus of chapter 12 is to recognize the Spirit's unique role in gifting the church rather than provide a review or explanation of each gift. Having said that, there does appear to be a way to categorize the gifts, depending upon the passage where they appear. The listing in Romans gives a group of practical gifts, including prophecy, serving, teaching, exhortation, giving, leadership, and mercy (Rom. 12:6-8). These are all gifts that focus on the practical needs of other people and are desperately needed in the church.

While all of the spiritual gifts are given to believers super-naturally, the gift list in 1 Corinthians 12 includes supernatural gifts that strike as more, well, supernatural. For instance, when we compare the gifts of serving and leadership in Romans to the gifts of tongues and the word of knowledge in 1 Corinthians, we recognize immediately the difference in essence in the two types of gifts. The list in 1 Corinthians includes those gifts that are usually deemed more common in the charismatic branches of the family tree. These include the utterance of wisdom, utterance of knowledge, faith, healing, miracles, prophecy, distinguishing of spirits, tongues, and the interpretation of tongues (vv. 8-11). To those gifts, Paul added a list of gifted offices, or people, who are spiritual gifts to the church. These include apostles, prophets, and teachers. A portion of the second list in 1 Corinthians may be repetition from the first list. It includes workers of miracles, those with gifts of healing, those who help, administrators, and those who speak in tongues (vv. 28-30). The debates about what gifts are operable in today's church usually center on the lists in 1 Corinthians rather than the list in Romans.

A third list, also gathered by Paul, is in Ephesians and is sim-ilar to the second list mentioned in 1 Corinthians. The Ephesians list is made up exclusively of gifted people who served in lead-ership capacities in the early church. This list includes apostles, prophets, evangelists, pastors, and teachers (4:11). These gifted leaders exist to "equip the saints for the work of ministry" (v. 12).

A short, fourth list found in 1 Peter 4 is interesting, because it may serve as an excellent way to think about all the gifts at once by viewing them as coming from one of two possible cat-egories. Peter said, "As each has received a gift, use it to serve one another, as good stewards of God's varied grace: whoever speaks, as one who speaks oracles of God; whoever serves, as one who serves by the strength that God supplies—in order that in everything God may be glorified through Jesus Christ. To him belong glory and dominion forever and ever. Amen" (vv. 10-11). Peter mentioned two categories of gifts: speaking gifts and serving gifts. When we study all the spiritual gifts mentioned in Scripture, we notice that most of them naturally fit into one of two categories: speaking gifts or serving gifts. Teachers and prophets have speaking gifts. People gifted in mercy or giving have serving gifts, and so on. Over many years of observation, I have seen how believers are usually tilted one way or the other. For instance, those with serving gifts are not usually also gifted with the speaking gifts; and those with the speaking gifts don't usually excel in the serving gifts. There may be exceptions to this principle, but generally we notice believers fitting more obviously and prominently in one gift category than the other.

The Spirit Gives Personal Gifts (vv. 4, 12-21)

The gifts of the Spirit are not generic or one-size-fits-all. That's good, since we don't always get the personal touch in life. We can easily feel that we are just one in seven billion others who are remarkably similar to us. I wasn't feeling the love, for instance, the day I received a piece of mail addressed to "Kie Bowman or Current Occupant"! The Holy Spirit doesn't give us gifts marked "Current Occupant." He has specific gifts for us.

Paul explained it to the Corinthians this way: "Now there are varieties of gifts, but the same Spirit" (v. 4). The word "varieties" is a Greek word coming from two words meaning literally "to take apart" or "to divide." The idea of the word conveys *differences*. Paul based much of his explanation about spiritual gifts on this distinction: not all gifts are the same. In fact, God's will is that a multiplicity of gifts would be in operation in the local church. To demonstrate his point, Paul used the human body as an illustration (vv. 12-20).

In these verses, Paul's example of the body as a metaphor for spiritual gifts is at the same time both brilliant and hilarious. He asks his readers to imagine the various parts of the human body in a family argument. In his imaginative illustration, feet can talk and think and have drawn the conclusion they are of no value because they aren't hands! Paul carries the absurdity of the illustration even further by introducing us to talking ears that complain they aren't happy and fulfilled because they aren't eyes. He asks us to imagine the tragic tale of an ear with an almost suicidal tendency because it no longer finds a reason to identify with the body, since, obviously, ears can't see!

We might expect Paul to ease up after the initial point is made, but he drills down further by fantasizing about an eye who complains that a hand is a useless appendage since it can't see. When we are tempted to say, "Paul, we get it," he continues by relaying the message that the head is fatigued at the thought of the uneducated and usually boorish feet (vv. 12-21).

This bizarre rant is a flight into the genius of Paul. He was writing to a combative and churlish congregation who had divided up among themselves like rivals in the Final Four, hoping to eliminate the competition. One group identified with Peter, another with Apollos, a third group were in Paul's camp, and a fourth—presumably those who considered themselves the most spiritually elite—were the Jesus faction (1:10-13). Paul drove home the absurdity of our competitive divisions within the church by an equally absurd picture of talking toes, hands with inferiority complexes, eyes with a superiority complex, and feet that feel underappreciated and unwanted!

The point of it all is this: We need each other; and our Spirit-gifted differences contribute to something larger than ourselves, just as the individual parts contribute to the functioning of the entire human body. The variety of gifts does not contribute to the chaos of competitive tribalism; instead, the differences are essential to the health of the entire church (v. 19). We are gifted differently because we have different roles to play in the church. This is not always easy for us to accept.

Winning the lost to Christ is a good ministry. Few things in life are more rewarding than explaining the gospel and watching the Lord transform a life. In a very real sense, everyone who shares their faith should be considered an evangelist. Still, the description is reserved for only one person in the New Testament—Phillip—who had previously served tables in the early church (Acts 21:8).

An evangelist in the New Testament was a gifted minister in the church. In the same way, apostles, prophets, pastors, and teachers were gifted ministers with specific roles (Eph. 4:11-12). Every believer is called to be a witness, but not all have the gift of the evangelist. The evangelist is unusually gifted by the Spirit to share the gospel clearly and lead others to faith in Christ. That's why it was a hard conversation when a young minister invited me for coffee to share his frustration. He wanted to be an evangelist like Billy Graham, but he confided that he never got invitations to preach. He was determined to serve the church as a vocational evangelist and wanted my thoughts on why the doors of opportunity had never opened for him. I asked a few questions and learned something revealing: never in his life had he led another person to Christ. He was seminary trained, had served in a few church jobs, and unquestionably loved the Lord. But, my friend, he was no evangelist. He seemed to have no gifting as an evangelist at all. Evangelists, both men and women, lead lost people to the Lord. They are gifted by the Spirit with that anointing. Not all those with the gift of the evangelist are preachers, but all of them are effective soul winners. My friend wanted to be like Billy Graham, but that was obviously not the Spirit's plan for his life.

> We are gifted differently because we have different roles to play in the church.

Sometimes believers, like my friend, become convinced they have a gift they do not possess, and the only result is frustration. Like the ear determined to be an eye, they spin their wheels spiritually and make no progress. Why? The answer is simple: spiritual gifts are distributed by the Holy Spirit (1 Cor. 12:4). God knows what He wants each of us to do; and, as a friend of mine humorously explained, "Even if a foot declares in faith it's an eye, reads books about being an eye, and attends conferences about being an eye, the only thing it's ever going to see is the inside of a sock, because it's a foot!" In other words, the Spirit may assign each of us one gift or several. He develops those gifts within us as we exercise and grow in the gifts, and He uses us to bless others through their use. The church desperately needs us to accept the Spirit's plan, in regard to the assignment of gifts, and serve others happily in the gift the Holy Spirit empowers us to use.

Identifying Your Gifts

The following thoughts about discovering your gifts are practical applications gleaned from pastoral ministry, studying the subject, and from personally walking with the Lord. Every believer should weigh his beliefs about his own gifts from the teachings of Scripture, in the crucible of real-life experiences, and from honest insights gathered from the wise counsel of godly people. So, how do we determine what gifts we have been given?

Do Everything. No job in the church is beneath any of us. When you are trying to find your gifts, you should volunteer for everything because your gift may become obvious as you serve. By the same token, you may do some tasks in ministry and sense no gifting at all, while those around you seem energized when doing the same things. In other words, while we are serving we begin to notice what we are drawn to and seem to do most effectively, or we notice the opposite. This is often an early clue to our gifting. Serving in your spiritual gifts is one of the most rewarding aspects of the Christian life. My dear wife, Tina, and I are a classic example. She excels in serving gifts and mine all fall in the category of speaking gifts. I can teach the Word—I love to get in front of anyone—from one person interested in growing in Christ to thousands gathered at a conference. I am energized by teaching and preaching, regardless of the size of the congregation. My wife, on the other hand, is filled with helping gifts and almost exclusively focuses her attention on ministry away from the spotlights. People are gifted differently, but we don't usually know that until we try a variety of ministries.

Seek the Counsel of Others. In the body of Christ, people will tell you what you need to know. When you notice other believers affirming you for certain tasks, pay attention. The Lord may be using them to tell you where your gifts are strongest. At our church we like to say: The man doesn't seek the job; the job seeks the man.

Read God's Word. What does the Bible say? Years ago, when I was just getting started in my walk with God, I didn't know what God wanted me to do. At a church service one night, when the preacher read his text, it was as if a lightning bolt struck my soul! I knew instinctively the passage he read was a description of my spiritual gifts. I felt electrified with excitement by the thought of it. That was nearly forty years ago, and it has been borne out as being authentic in hundreds of ministry hours since that time. God will tell you your gifts if you will prayerfully read and listen to His Word.

Gift Tests. Most churches provide their members with spiritual gift inventories, which are usually extremely helpful. Ask one of your pastors about such a tool.

Walk in the Spirit. Ultimately, most things in the Christian life are more accessible when we are living in humble obedience to the Lord. The closer we are to His heart, the more likely we'll be to sense His purpose for our lives. Have you sought the infilling of the Holy Spirit? The gifts are a manifestation of the Spirit, so seek a nearness to Him and the fullness of the Spirit to activate His gifts.

Suit Up

Do you like sports? Football is king where I live. The church I serve is about twenty blocks from the University of Texas, and we have an excellent view of the huge, beautiful stadium where the Texas Longhorns play. Most people I know love football.

Even though I'm a Texas Longhorn football fan, my real love is the NBA—the National Basketball Association. I grew up loving basketball. I watch a lot of games on television, especially during the playoffs. There is something about basketball—from school sports all the way to the NBA—that reminds me of spiritual gifts in the body of Christ.

At all times five players from my team are on the floor playing the game. Players in the NBA are tall. In fact, the average height is 6 feet, 7 inches—almost a foot taller than the average American man—with power forwards and centers averaging 6 feet, 11 inches.[1] While not always the case, the shortest player on the court is often the point guard. Sometimes the best point guards are nearly a foot shorter than most of the other players. Think of former players John Stockton, Steve Nash, or Derek Fisher. They are all visibly shorter than their teammates. Think about the superstar point guards who are playing at the time of this writing: Steph Curry, Chris Paul, or Isaiah Thomas. They are also significantly shorter than most of their teammates. Isaiah Thomas is listed as only about 5 feet, 9 inches. Yet, in spite of the height difference of these players as compared to most of the other players on the floor, the point guards are usually the floor generals of the team. They control the pace, have possession of the ball most often, and run the plays.

Then there is a group of players known as shooting guards. They are high-percentage scoring machines. They must wake up every morning with the same thought running through their minds: Give me the ball, I'm feeling it! Every team needs shooting guards.

Often less celebrated by casual observers are the players who don't score as many points; but their size, basketball IQ, and athleticism makes them great defenders. They block shots, snag rebounds, and frustrate the other team's offense. The big, powerful defenders are essential to winning.

Of course, everyone loves to watch the seven-foot giants who devastate their opponents inside the paint. These centers—the *Big Men* of the team—can slam a dunk so hard they rattle the backboards and their opponent's confidence with equal dexterity.

Each player on the floor is different. They serve different functions. They think differently. They play different roles on the team. All of them, however, have the same objective: they want to win the game. Basketball is a team sport, so everyone is needed to win.

The church that is empowered by the Holy Spirit, and operating in their spiritual gifts, reminds me of a winning team. Our gifts are different. We think differently about how we approach ministries. Our functions differ. Our objective, however, remains the same. We want to serve God, reach the world for Christ, and minister to our fellow believers. In order to do this effectively, we need everyone to "suit up for the game" and use their spiritual gifts to contribute what they can.

God designed the church to operate in the supernatural manifestation of the Holy Spirit through the use of our spiritual gifts. We need everyone to be involved. The stakes are high, and we are running out of time. We need you and your spiritual gifts—now.

1 "Male Body Image and the Average Athlete," PsychGuides.com: An American Addictions Center Resource, accessed December 5, 2018, https://www.psychguides.com/interact/male-body-image-and-the-average-athlete/.

8

THE SPIRIT PROTECTS
THE CHURCH

Ephesians 1:13-14

D o you feel safe? Most Americans do not. In spite of the fact crime rates have been reduced drastically since their peak in the early 1990s, Americans continue, year after year, to tell pollsters that crime has increased since the previous year.[1] While crime rates go down, we imagine they are going up. Are we an insecure culture?

Even though statistics tell us we are less likely to be crime victims than in previous decades, real crime does happen, and it's not an easy thing to forget. In fact, there's nothing easy about being the intended target of a crime.

When I was a teenager our home was burglarized, and I still remember how it affected everyone in my family. My brother and I came home from school one afternoon in the middle of winter and found several things out of place. We are from Alaska, so it was brutally cold outside—maybe thirty degrees below zero—and dark, as it was every day in the winter by that time of day. When we walked in the front door, the house was weirdly drafty and cold. Immediately we saw that all the drawers of the built-in living room cabinets were wide open. My brother said correctly, "Something is not right here."

I walked to the back of the house to find the back door standing open, as subzero temperatures blew icy wind into the house. We walked beside our parents' bedroom and saw that Dad's guns had been taken out of the case, down from the rack, and were on the bed. We had been burglarized.

We immediately called our parents, who were both still at work. My mother broke down in tears. Someone called the police, and Dad and Mom were home quickly. The police said the guns on the bed, the back door standing wide open, and the pattern of the footprints in the snow that indicated the perpetrator was running when he left all pointed to the fact the intruder must have been in the house when my brother and I walked up the driveway. Our loud talking and laughing and our key in the lock startled the thief, who must have run immediately out the back door. When my mother heard that her two sons had probably walked in on a robbery in progress, she was inconsolable. I had never seen her like that before. She kept thinking about what might have happened.

God has sent the Holy Spirit to protect us until we go to heaven.

Being robbed is a terrible thing. You are left feeling vulnerable; and, like my mom, you can't help wondering how much worse things might have been. Maybe that's one reason so many people feel unsafe. Maybe they remember the old days when things were worse.

The crime rates aren't as bad as they once were, but there are other kinds of dangers today, and the frequency and severity of the incidents seem to be getting worse. Many twenty-first-century Christians, for instance, talk about threats against religious liberty. For example, Greg Laurie wrote, "The church is under attack as never before. It is under attack around the world, and it is under attack in our own country. Christians are summarily mocked, marginalized, and dismissed as lunatics. Overseas, our brothers and sisters are being martyred by Islamic terrorists and Communists. It is enough to cause Christians to become downright discouraged."[2]

History shows the church has often been attacked. Christians have been jailed, tortured, driven underground, and their churches destroyed; yet Christianity continues to grow and spread around the world. How has the church survived and grown in spite of all of the persecution it has endured through the centuries? And why do we so often remain faithful when we are physically attacked by enemies of the gospel or attacked spiritually through temptation and satanic oppression?

Believers are confident because the Holy Spirit promises to protect us. None of us should presume we are strong enough on our own to survive every potential threat to our soul. Our enemy is ruthless; and our faith, we must admit, is sometimes weak. But God has sent the Holy Spirit to help us live the Christian life, give us courage to fight our spiritual battles, and protect us until we go to heaven.

Spiritual Security Detail

One of my friends is retired from the Secret Service. On March 30, 1981, the day President Ronald Reagan was shot, my friend was working at the next planned stop in the president's security detail. In fact, my friend was assigned the responsibility of serving as the security detail at President Reagan's hospital room while he was recuperating.

We expect our leaders to be protected. They're important to us as a nation, and we want them to have an excellent security detail. We protect what we care about, and God is the same way. He protects what belongs to Him. The Spirit provides spiritual protection for our salvation, even better than law enforcement can provide physical protection to every citizen all the time.

Have you ever considered what it cost the Lord to give life to the church? Jesus left heaven and became a fragile embryo in a virgin womb. He was born into a poor, small-town family where hard work was all they knew. We are told little about His life for the first thirty years, until He began His public ministry. Within three years He was persecuted by the religious establishment, until He was sentenced to die at the hands of the Roman government.

His death was brutal. He was beaten so badly it might appear somewhat surprising that He didn't die from the blood loss and trauma. Then He was nailed to the cross. Within six hours He was dead. Of course, our Gospels go on to explain He was buried and was raised to life again on the third day.

Even after Jesus's resurrection, His scars and unhealed wounds from the crucifixion were still visible. All of this was done so you and I could be saved. God loves us so much He sent Jesus to live a difficult life, die a horrible death, and leave the unfinished work of world evangelization to us.

Let me ask you a question: Do you think after Jesus was willing to do all that—suffering as He did in order to give us life— He would just say, "Good luck now!"? Would He simply tell us to take our best shot at getting to heaven? Would He walk away and leave us alone, knowing we'll be left to fight devils throughout life and endure suffering for His sake, simply because His crucifixion was complete and He wanted to get back to heaven?

Of course not; after all, He sacrificed Himself in order to save us. He made provision to protect what He redeemed. The Holy Spirit protects what the Lord Jesus has saved. Our souls are kept safe by the Spirit.

For the rest of your life you will be the devil's target. He hates God. He hates the plan of God. He hates the church of God. I hope you're not surprised when I say the devil hates you. As a result of Satan's fury against everything God wants to bless, you will face temptations and spiritual warfare all of your life. Since God wants to use you to advance the Kingdom, the enemy views you as a threat, and he's right—you are a threat! So how are you going to survive the onslaught of hell against you? Are you going to be determined and strong-willed enough to defeat the devil? No. The highway of history is littered with the remains of determined men who were no match for the weaponized, energized, satanic onslaughts of hell. You need more than yourself to fight this battle. Your soul is at stake, and you are the possession of the King. He has left you here, but you were not left alone. The Holy Spirit is your security detail!

Protection

Your salvation matters so much to God He makes certain the Holy Spirit protects it. We find this truth clearly revealed in Ephesians 1:3-14, which is the longest sentence in the Greek New Testament. Obviously, the translators apply the appropriate punctuation so these verses make the most sense in English; but in the original language it's just one long, spiraling, brilliant sentence.

For that reason, to understand any part of it, wisdom insists we view each part of this marathon sentence in light of the entire thought Paul expressed. The theme of the whole is God's planning, purchase, and protection of your salvation to the praise of His glory.

The passage is divided into three sections, with each division devoted to one part of the Trinity. The conclusion of each individual section, and the transition to the next, is marked by these phrases: "to the praise of his glorious grace" (v. 6), "to the praise of his glory" (v. 12), and, again, "to the praise of his glory" (v. 14). This is more than a well-planned, literary device. Paul allows no confusion about the source or the substance of salvation. We take no credit for our redemption. God is responsible for our deliverance from start to finish "to the praise of his glory."

Father (vv. 3-6)

In the first section of this passage, Paul pulls back the curtain of eternity and shows us God the Father's hand in planning the salvation of His people. We are told we have been chosen "before the foundation of the world" (v. 4), His predestined and adopted people through Jesus for His own purposes (v. 5). The takeaway from this section is clear: God planned our salvation.

Son (vv. 6-12)

What the Father planned, the Son purchased! The second section of Paul's explanation focuses on the price of our salvation, paid by the Lord Jesus. We have "redemption through his blood" (v. 7). Through His sacrifice, Jesus became the way for us to be forgiven and the revelation of the Father's will (vv. 7-9). In the Lord Jesus, heaven and earth are being reunited, and our inheritance from the Father is found in the Son (vv. 10-11). In this section of the "salvation sentence," Paul extols the virtue of the Son, His sacrifice, and all He has done to purchase our redemption.

The Holy Spirit (vv. 13-14)

The Holy Spirit protects the salvation of Christ's followers. Paul tells us the Spirit has "sealed" the souls of those who trust in Christ: "In him you also, when you heard the word of truth, the gospel of your salvation, and believed in him, were sealed with the promised Holy Spirit, who is the guarantee of our inheritance until we acquire possession of it, to the praise of his glory" (vv. 13-14). Have you ever thought about the fact the church is "sealed"? It means the salvation of every believer is protected. Why does Paul use the concept of being sealed by the Holy Spirit? What does it signify?

The word *sealed*, in the original language, comes from a root word meaning "to fence in or to close up." It carries the idea of protecting an asset. I need a fence around my backyard to keep my dog from running freely and, perhaps, getting into trouble. My fence also keeps the deer from eating our flowers and the cauliflower my wife is growing. So my fence protects my *assets* by keeping my dog in and keeping the local deer out. In a similar way, the Holy Spirit protects my soul by keeping unwanted intruders away, and His presence and influence keeps me from wandering away. We will look more deeply at these two ideas later in this chapter. For now, let's understand how the word *sealed* is used and understood.

The Holy Spirit protects the salvation of Christ's followers.

Over time, "sealed" started to mean a way of describing authority. For instance, when the Roman governor Pontius Pilate wanted to secure the stone in front of the entrance to Jesus's borrowed tomb, it was sealed (Matt. 27:65-66). The seal was an inscription—probably of Rome—imprinted or pressed into a soft, moldable substance, possibly clay, which was affixed across the stone with some kind of rope or cord.[3] The seal itself was simple and easy to break, but the empire it represented was the most powerful in the world.

When you send an old-fashioned envelope across the country, you seal it. The seal is paper and inexpensive glue. The contents of the letter may be of a highly personal nature. The envelope may contain a check or contracts with your social security number and other personal information written inside, or you might even, on rare occasions, send cash. The paper and cheap glue used to seal the letter are not sufficient in themselves to protect the contents; but the laws of the United States Government regarding mail tampering are usually enough to protect your stuff.

Violating the Roman seal across Jesus's tomb meant disobeying the same government that had crucified an innocent man for political purposes only a few hours earlier. The implication was clear—the seal bore the mark of authority. The word used in Matthew for sealing the tomb is the same one used to describe the Spirit's protection of believers. The Holy Spirit has the God-given authority to protect that which Jesus ransomed with His blood.

The same word is also used to describe a seal in the sense of a visible marking. For instance, in the book of Revelation the Lord puts some kind of distinguishing mark on the foreheads of His chosen servants (7:3). The clear teaching of the passage in Revelation is the guaranteed safety of God's servants, as evidenced by the seal. If God seals it—whatever it is—it is secured!

The idea of the Holy Spirit sealing the believers is not obscure in Paul's writings. In fact, he actually returns to the concept on more than one occasion to describe the protection afforded to the believer as a result of the Holy Spirit's ministry. To the Corinthians, Paul again uses the illustration of the seal to point to the believer's security: "And it is God who establishes us with you in Christ, and has anointed us, and who has also put his seal on us and given us his Spirit in our hearts as a guarantee" (2 Cor. 1:21-22). When you are sealed with the Holy Spirit, as Paul said, you possess the inheritance of the family as a kind of down payment. Everything coming to you is already yours, and the Holy Spirit is the current evidence of the coming blessings.

Queen Elizabeth II is the longest-serving monarch in British royal history. Her son Prince Charles has always popularly been considered the heir to the throne, but it was not until April 2018 the succession plan was officially approved by the Commonwealth heads of state and government. At the time of this writing, Prince Charles is enjoying the fact he will be king at some point. He is not king yet; but in the minds of the rest of the world, it is inevitable. He is king—almost. He has the monarchy—but not yet.[4] In a somewhat related way, all the benefits of heaven and eternal life have been granted to the followers of Christ. We possess everything already—but not yet. The Holy Spirit is the guarantee of our eventual, full inheritance.

The seal of the Spirit is repeated again in Ephesians 4, where we are instructed to not "grieve the Holy Spirit of God, by whom you were sealed for the day of redemption" (v. 30). Paul knew the seal of the Spirit on our lives would protect us until we got to heaven on "the day of redemption."

The Down Payment (v. 14)

Another form of the protection provided by the Holy Spirit is what Paul called "the guarantee of our inheritance" (v. 14). We have already mentioned the concept earlier in this chapter, since Paul had made the same observation about the Holy Spirit's ministry when he encouraged the Corinthians (2 Cor. 1:21-22).

The word *guarantee* used in Ephesians is the equivalent idea of our concept of a down payment. I understand down payments.

When I got out of high school, before college, I went to work selling cars at a local import dealership in my hometown. One day two men walked in and asked me about the price of our popular-selling pickup trucks. When I quoted the price of a new truck, they informed me they were buying a *fleet* of trucks, and they wanted the best deal. That day, as an eighteen-year-old salesman who worked on commission, I sold sixteen new pickup trucks to one customer! It was a good day. In order for me to *hold* the vehicles while they arranged final payment and before they could take possession, they wrote a check to the dealership as a *down payment*. That meant the other salesmen couldn't sell the trucks, even though the new owners hadn't finished all the transaction paperwork. Their down payment was large enough to show they were serious buyers, and no one could have those trucks but them. In that way, the trucks, while not yet in their possession, were *off the market* from other buyers. The down payment *protected* the trucks as theirs until the day came when they could take them.

> The Spirit Himself is the guarantee of all that God has prepared for His people.

Imagine everything God has promised to the church when we are finally in heaven. It is beyond our wildest imaginations (1 Cor. 2:9). Still, because of the Holy Spirit, we are already enjoying heaven on earth. The Spirit Himself is the guarantee of all that God has prepared for His people. More than that, since the Spirit is a guarantee, He is protecting us until we arrive safely to our final reward. God has taken possession of us by securing what is His with a down payment.

Why Do We Need Protection?

Our salvation needs protection because we have an enemy. His objective is to destroy the works of God, and that includes harming us (John 10:10). If we were left without protection, we would not survive. Our salvation would be vulnerable to the predator who seeks only our harm.

In addition, we are not completely reliable. If we are left to ourselves, how long will our salvation be secure? I know me, so I'm glad I've got a protector. The Holy Spirit watches over all of the people of God. He protects what Jesus has bought with His blood.

When I was growing up I lived down the block from a family with several brothers. They had a strong family resemblance. I always had the feeling, if you had seen one you had seen them all. They were a tough bunch of kids. Fights were common. Everyone knew if one of the little brothers got into a fight, their older brothers would somehow appear on the scene. Most kids knew if you fought one you might have to fight all of them. That fact kept the little brothers out of trouble—most of the time.

If I was left alone, I would be an easy target for the enemy of my soul. Not only that, I can be inconsistent and weaker than I want to be. The good news is, when I am weak or under spiritual attack, I've got a kind of "big brother" who comes to my defense. The Holy Spirit always protects the people of God.

---

1 John Gramlich, "5 Facts about Crime in the U.S.," FactTank, Pew Research Center, January 30, 2018, http://www.pewresearch.org/fact-tank/2018/01/30/5-facts-about-crime-in-the-u-s/.

2 Greg Laurie, "It's Time To Fight Back," Harvest, July 10, 2018, https://harvest.org/resources/devotion/its-time-to-fight-back/.

3 "Christ's Tomb Is Sealed," Ligonier Ministries, accessed December 10, 2018, https://www.ligonier.org/learn/devotionals/christs-tomb-sealed/.

4 Caroline Halleman, "Prince Charles to Succeed Queen Elizabeth as Head of the Commonwealth," *Town & Country* magazine, April 20, 2018, https://www.townandcountrymag.com/society/tradition/a19861527/prince-charles-head-commonwealth/.

EPILOGUE

A Personal Relationship with the Spirit

God wants you to be filled with the Holy Spirit (Eph. 5:18). God wants you to walk in the Spirit (Gal. 5:16). God wants you to live by the Spirit (Gal. 5:25).

Every follower of Jesus should have a deeply personal relationship with the Holy Spirit. In order to assist you in developing that relationship, therefore, I invite you to consider two passages from the teachings of Jesus and the apostle Paul.

Paul had already referred to the ministry of the Holy Spirit at least eight times in Ephesians before he urged them to be filled with the Spirit (Eph. 1:13; 2:18, 22; 3:5, 16; 4:3-4, 30). This constant conversation about the Spirit's ministry undergirds the theme of this book; namely, the ministry of the Spirit isn't limited to only the exciting personal issue of fullness in the Spirit. The believer should, however, seek fullness in the Spirit as the Scripture teaches.

The word *filled* is important for our consideration. The Greek word used means "to be completely full or filled to the top." It is a word that conjures the idea of a vase or bucket filled to the point of overflowing with the liquid poured into it. That's what the Spirit does. He fills every corner of our lives. He leaves nothing empty that can be filled. He chases away everything that competes for preeminence in our lives, and He fills us to the brim!

EMPOWERED

Paul teaches at least four things in Ephesians 5:18 about being filled with the Spirit that help us understand what God wants for every believer. Let's look closely at this important passage in the Word of God: "And do not get drunk with wine, for that is debauchery, but be filled with the Spirit" (Eph. 5:18).

1. God's Will for You

First, the instruction to "be filled with the Spirit" is built on a verb phrase: "be filled." This verb in the Greek text is an imperative, which means the action stated is a command. This leaves no room for excuses. The Spirit-filled life is not an optional approach to the Christian life. It's not just for *other* believers. The Spirit-filled life is commanded for *every* believer. That means living the Spirit-filled life is a matter of obedience to the Lordship of Jesus Christ.

2. God's Will Now

The second thing of interest about the verb phrase "be filled" is its tense. It is a present tense verb. This fact implies at least two things: First, no believer should delay seeking the fullness of the Spirit. God wants you to be filled with the Spirit now! Second, we should walk in the fullness of the Spirit at all times. Our experience of fullness doesn't come and go with circumstances; we are to live in the present tense of the Spirit-filled life.

3. God Does the Filling

A third informative detail found in the phrase "be filled" has to do with who is performing the action. In other words, who is doing the filling? The verb is passive, meaning you do not fill yourself. Instead, you are filled. Think about it. The Spirit-filled life isn't a matter of *your* effort. Instead, it is a gracious work of God in your life.

4. God's Plan for All of Us

The fourth factor to consider about the Spirit-filled life and the phrase "be filled" has to do with who is invited to experience the Spirit. The verb is plural. A correct literal translation could be "you all be filled." In other words, the Spirit-filled life isn't offered to a small group of church leaders or to a few denominations. Paul was writing to an entire congregation. God wants everyone in the body of Christ to be filled with the Holy Spirit!

Have you experienced the Spirit-filled life? Do you want to experience it? The next passage to consider comes from the Lord Jesus. In Luke's Gospel, Jesus was teaching His followers to pray, and He gave us a promise regarding the Spirit-filled life: "If you then, who are evil, know how to give good gifts to your children, how much more will the heavenly Father give the Holy Spirit to those who ask him!" (11:13).

In this passage Jesus describes the goodness of God. He says the child of God who desires the Holy Spirit's presence in life should ask God for the gift of the Holy Spirit. Of course, it's true that every Christian already has the Holy Spirit in his or her life; but it is also true that God invites us to press in for a fullness of the Spirit. The simplest way to experience what God has for us, according to Jesus, is to pray. We ask, and He provides.

Consider a simple prayer right now. "Lord, please fill me with the Holy Spirit."

More from the Discipleship Collection

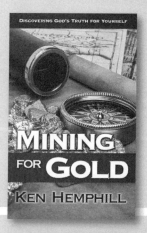

Do you believe God's truth is more precious than gold? Do you dig into God's Word with the same passion you would exert to find physical gold? Learn three different styles of reading and eight essential questions to ask of every text to help you discover the pure riches of God's Word.

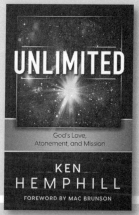

This study of the love, atonement, and mission of God addresses the crucial issue of the extent of the gospel and who can respond to the good news. It will encourage every person to confidently join Unlimited God in His Kingdom mission to redeem the peoples of the whole world.

For teaching guides and additional small group study materials, or to learn about other Auxano Press titles, visit Auxanopress.com.